BREAK THE HUSTLE BARRIER

Growing Your Business from Mere Hustle to a Profitable Venture

Morenike Ogunnowo

Copyright 2021 © **Morenike Ogunnowo**

All rights reserved.

No part of this book may be reproduced, distributed, stored or transmitted in any form or by any means, including electronic, photocopy, recording, reproducing or resale without the prior written permission of the author and publisher, except in the case of brief quotations embodied in reviews and articles as well as certain other non-commercial uses permitted by copyright law.

DEDICATION

I dedicate this book to the Almighty, the All-Knowing and my ONLY sufficient God for the grace I enjoy through His mercy.

I also dedicate this to my dear parents, Mr Olukayode Adekoya and Mrs Funmilayo Adekoya. You both gave me what money could not buy.

My special dedication goes to the husband of my youth, Pastor Adeola Gbenga Ogunnowo, for being supportive and to my kids for their consistent understanding.

ACKNOWLEDGEMENTS

I am thankful to God for being the true source of inspiration and giver of knowledge. Over the years, He has made the journey of life an opportunity for me to inspire others and been at the heart of all businesses that effectively work with His principles. His instruction and guidance have enabled me to impact others through knowledge.

I want to specially thank the team that worked with me on this project. Mrs Adedolapo Ebadan, my outstanding editor, thank you for giving the book an excellent touch and making it worth reading. You are more of a sister than an editor to me. Jerry Kanyinebi, thank you for the beautiful cover design you made and your profound advice over the course of the project. You are great at what you do. Temitope Oluwanifemi Emmanuel, thank you for that gracious hand of support. Your good heart speaks for you. I appreciate you so much.

My appreciation also goes to my immediate family – Pastor Adeola Gbenga Ogunnowo (husband), Emmanuel Ogunnowo (son), Favour Ogunnowo (daughter), Joanna and John Ogunnowo (our twins) – for being understanding. It is obvious that they were created for my world, given their cooperation during the writing of this book. They made wifely and maternal duties easy for me. My husband, particularly, is a friend, my spiritual father and my number one fan whose words of encouragement instil the "I can" attitude in me at all times. I appreciate the way you love me.

My parents, guardians, and support, thank you for being there while I was studying to become a certified professional accountant at university. You eased my academic journey there and made the experience one of the best things that have ever happened to me. I thank you for believing in my dream, for the provision when it was obvious you did not have enough and for the word of wisdom that shaped my sense of reasoning. The industry, which I learnt from you while I was growing up, comes in handy in situations I find myself now. I am eternally indebted to you for giving me what money cannot buy.

I also want to appreciate my immediate siblings, Omotayo Adekoya (elder brother) and Oluwatosin Adekoya (younger brother) and step siblings, Jumoke Adekoya, Deyemi Adekoya, Tope Adekoya and others. You all gave me the experiences that make me unique today.

To every staff member who worked with me in my businesses at one point or the other, I say a big thank you. You all made my entrepreneurial experience worth its while. Olaitan Suru and Oludare Sulaiman and others, yourloyalty and support to my business go beyond what I employed you for. I cannot forget you so easily. To every other person who is instrumental in the experience I gather as a business owner, you are very much appreciated.

I cannot forget a former colleague turned sister, Omobabinrin Adeola Osideko (FCCA). Even though we do not work together any longer in the same company, the relationship we have built over the years inspired the early completion of this project. You clearly demonstrated how real you are and took it upon yourself to care about my progress, confirming the wise saying that the people you have around you determine how far you can easily see or go. This acknowledgement would not be complete without a mention of your impact.

To all the great coaches I met in the journey of personal development, I say a big thank to you. You made me the person I am today, thanks to the much you poured into my life. Omolara Ogun, Uzo Nwankwo and many others, thank you for your immense contributions to my person, especially with your vast knowledge which rubbed off on me throughout my stay at KPMG Professional Services.

Messrs Toba Emmanuel Adesanwo, Emeka Nobis, Akinola Akinboboye, Ayo Adelakun, Kunle Koleosho and many others, thank you for the knowledge you professionally delivered in my professional journey. Katsuhiro Murooka and other MDs that I have been privileged to work with, thanks for your willingness to teach me many work-related concepts. My colleagues at Honda Manufacturing Nigeria Limited, thank you for creating platforms for me to shine and the experience working with you has brought.

To all my business class enrollees, thank you for helping me to sharpen my understanding in my chosen field through coaching. Tolulope Ajayi, Nimi Adetiran and Bunmi Onabanjo, I cannot forget your willingness to learn. You are sisters in the true definition of it. Thank you for making coaching easy. To many others that have allowed me to share knowledge with you, you are all appreciated.

God has blessed me with the gift of men. I appreciate everyone who has contributed to my experience, which forms the basis of writing this book. Thank you so much.

To you holding this book at this time and everyone who will read and apply its contents, I sincerely appreciate you. You are the real MVP (Most Valuable Person). You are greatly loved.

FOREWORD

Morenike Ogunnowo and I have been best of friends for about two decades, having met at the University. When she informed me of her desire to have me write the Foreword of her book, I was very pleased for several reasons. First, I was impressed that my good friend could find time to write such an inspiring piece despite her extremely busy schedule as a Chief Financial Officer of a multinational and an entrepreneur. Secondly, I wanted to be one of the first to read the book and learn from her thoughts, experience, and inspiration as an entrepreneur, especially in a tough environment like Nigeria.

Morenike has always been a "hustler" from our university days. Though we were not in the same department but were bound by the Institute of Chartered Accountants of Nigeria (ICAN) exam lecture classes and were attracted to each other's dedication and determination to succeed. Since we left the university and qualified as chartered accountants, she has never disappointed me in my expectations of her dexterity as a core professional and her prowess for entrepreneurship.

The book "Break the Hustle Barrier" perfectly speaks of the reality of the Nigerian phenomenon. The system is saddled with more ratio of dependents to providers and these providers must find a way to increase their earning capacity, considering the level of underemployment and unemployment in the country, due to incompetence at the helms of affairs, corruption, impunity, and lack of empathy from our political leaders which have made most citizens to provide for everything for themselves and assume the role of the "state" in their own capacity.

With graduates now being encouraged to have entrepreneurial mindset to make a living in the current tough economic circumstance, I must say this book is a very good fit for purpose and a manual for economic liberation. Gone are the days graduates were expected to be too fixated and hopeful for employment, especially in Nigeria. This book will be very helpful in creating the right mindset in our teaming youth population in Nigeria and beyond. I believe that this is a useful tool in the hands of anyone who is willing to abide by the principles elaborated by Morenike as there are so many entrepreneurial opportunities around us.

My hope is that you will get as much inspiration from this book and gain from Morenike's personal entrepreneurial experience and inspiration to unleash the entrepreneurial skill in you as I have come to learn that entrepreneurial skills are not necessarily inborn but can be acquired with discipline, training, and determination.

Ayodeji Adelakun *FCA*
Lagos, Nigeria
14th February 2021

TABLE OF CONTENTS

DEDICATION   iv

ACKNOWLEDGEMENTS   v

FOREWORD   ix

INTRODUCTION   xii

Chapter 1 LESSONS FROM MY EXPERIENCE   15

Chapter 2 MINDSET SHIFT – ENTREPRENEURIAL MINDSET   29

Chapter 3 YOUR BUSINESS ENVIRONMENT SIMPLIFIED   41

Chapter 4 KNOWING JUST THE RIGHT STRATEGY FOR YOU 63

Chapter 5 MANAGING BUSINESS ASSETS FOR GROWTH   83

Chapter 6 WHAT I NEED TO KNOW ABOUT BUSINESS PLAN DEVELOPMENT   105

Chapter 7 PUTTING STRUCTURES IN PLACE   123

Chapter 8 SEEING YOUR NEXT 5 YEARS' PROFIT TODAY 135

Chapter 9 WHY YOU SHOULD KEEP A PROPER RECORD   145

Chapter 10 WHAT WOULD YOU DO DIFFERENTLY?   155

REFERENCES   176

INTRODUCTION

Break the Hustle Barrier is a precious gift to the world of business. The book is for existing and new startups whose businesses could either be their side gigs or core gigs. Inasmuch as you intend to make income from it, then it is necessary that you understand the business side of it.

While it is okay to think that being a hustler means you are very hardworking in making money to meet your immediate needs, there is need to start taking practical steps to liberate yourself and strengthening your resolve with the understanding of growing and efficient business operations.

Over the years, the word *hustle* has been misused by many people, including those who engage in unethical and dubious activities. I am sure you do not want to be categorised alongside this set of people. That is why you need to be mindful of your business growth. One major barrier that has been keeping several business owners from growing is their lack of understanding of what business is. This has to do with business education. The information on what business should be seen as has yet to be fully circulated. A lot of lies on what business is have been transferred from generation to generation, leaving only a few people who are ready to do the work and be different as key players in their respective industries. This is because challenges push a lot of people to start businesses and leave them with no choice but to earn from any available opportunity. They believe that when such opportunity comes, it is normal for them to take it on to make ends meet.

Nevertheless, many of them fail to gain the knowledge of business. In point of fact, your growth starts from your mindset. And until it changes, it will be difficult for you to grow. It is not enough for you to have the technical knowledge of your business; you need to have fundamental knowledge of how to operate the business.

I have, over the years, engaged with different people who intend to start their businesses or run existing businesses and seen a lot of gap in the approach they adopted in doing their businesses. Some have technically seen the money-making aspect of business as the only route, neglecting other areas that speak greatly about whether or not their businesses will continue as a "going concern." Confusion arises between acquisition of skills, product initiation and branding on one hand and engaging in ideal activities of business on the other hand. Other concerns stem from how business owners, out of this little knowledge or their nonchalance towards adopting the right approach to business, have lost control of theirbusinesses, resulting in the death of such businesses.

The aim of this book, therefore, is to guide new and existing business owners with basic information that they need to grow their businesses from mere hustle to profitable and sustainable ventures. Business success startsfrom how well the owners understand what they are doing in line with the right approaches they adopt to have sustainable businesses. No investor will be comfortable to deal with you if any of these fundamentals is missing. As you read this book, you will be exposed to all relevant topics for all businessmen and women who need to be equipped so that they can function effectively and be proud of their businesses.

Chapter 1

LESSONS FROM MY EXPERIENCE

Why did I choose to be in business? What motivated me to be in business? Perhaps you could be encouraged to do the right thing after reading my story. You might have asked yourself several questions about life. Be reliably informed that you are not the only person who has experienced what life brings. Perhaps you have questioned the reason for being in a difficult situation, the reason for things to have turned out the way they are in your business or the reason for making a decision that landed you in the business. Moving forward, you will learn from my story, which confirms that being in business is one of the best things you could choose for yourself. That is why I congratulate you for coming across this eye-opening book in times like this. Reading it will expose you to a lot of things that are peculiar to your business, which you have either started or have yet to start.

As a young woman with a career in its early days and in a young marriage years ago, I knew I needed more to maintain the standard of living that I wished for myself. Being an auditor at the time was time-consuming, as it left me with little time for myself and my family. Despite this limitation, I was convinced that there was more to do to help ME. I loved helping people, improving my performance through training, and taking care of myself in my own way.

Nevertheless, I could not fully explore this life, no thanks to my earnings then. Well, it could be the best for someone who was not at the same level in another company, excluding someone working in an oil company and whose paycheck is above a Big 4 accounting firm. The time I invested in the work based on requirements and its nature was quite much and only an accountant or auditor understands this.

Spending on a lot of things far outweighed my pay each month and that resulted in me taking up loans or an advance to get immediate needs with the obligation to pay from my salary in future. At some point, this became a cycle as I continued to borrow once I finished paying the previous ones. This led to me getting more occupied with work as I felt that the work would be my only saviour. Nevertheless, I got bored, especially when it appeared that the situation would not change.

Deep down, I was hungry for more money. I had fantasies for a blissful life. But if I had to continue that way, events did not show that anything needed to change.

Hardly had I started my marital journey than my husband resigned and started personal work and ministry assignment. It was a call he had to answer. I understood the whole situation and supported him fully. Eyebrows were raised at this time, especially by those who did not understand why I supported him. But I intentionally turned a deaf ear to naysayers to avoid something contrary to the joy I planned to have in my marriage. In the end, it turned out to be a wise decision, given that I kept away unnecessary negative and unhealthy influences during the period.

Why did I have to come to the level of starting a business? Yes, I was an employee when I started and I am still an employee. If you are an employee now, it is not enough reason why you should not have other businesses you are running. Having examined myself, the nature of my job and the environment in which the firm I worked in operated, I resorted to doing side gigs to make extra money. When I started, I fought the psychological battle of being looked down on as a salesperson when my career as an auditor was expected to be of high profile. How can an ACA be reduced to selling items? Won't my professionalism be doubted if found selling items? Answering these questions, I gave myself several reasons why I should not tell people that I was into sales of jewellery and other fashion items.

Some people believe that once you start a business, you should stick to it alone. Nevertheless, they forget that we are in a country where you have to do more than normal to keep your feet standing. Some time ago, in an entrepreneurship workshop organised by an insurance company, one of the facilitators turned me off when he stated that one should not have other sources of income if one is working in a company. I became uninterested in this claim because it does not agree with the reality of an average Nigerian worker.

Moreover, it came from someone who was not a Nigerian and who worked at the executive level of the company, a blue chip company at that. He had everything he needed on a platter. These made me conclude that he was talking from his perspective: the feeling that he was fulfilled in his own sense.

On the contrary, as Africans in general and Nigerians in particular, employment might not be the only thing you have to depend on to be financially liberated. So, while doing your side gig(s), it is important that you create a system that would not clash with the time you need to work for your employer. Your personal business system should not make you cheat your employer. You also have to upscale your time management skill. This is because this decision is not for the lazy.

As an employee who wants to have another business without cheating your employer, you need to have clarity on what you intend to do and plan your business such that there will not be conflict of interest. Also, it is ethically wrong for you, as an employee in a company, to deal in the same business as your employer. When this happens, there is no way you will be able to manage conflict of interest. Even if you do, you will be perceived as someone who does not. In business, your integrity is not to be confirmed by you alone; others must see you doing it.

As a newly-wed who needed money, I had to think outside the box and looked for what I could do while building my career. My workplace at the time was a place that kept me so busy that I would sometimes get home late. So, when it comes to time, I did not have the luxury of it. Despite this, I chose to create time out of none. Why? I looked at the income I mentioned and discovered it was not enough for me. So, I had to create such time to get something better for myself.

What did I do differently? I analysed the kind of business that could fit into the working environment. I pondered on a lot of things and asked several questions. I did a lot of research. In fact, my research went as far as investing a lot in the test run of some markets, suppliers and the like. If you know your way, you do not have to do that. Had it been I had this kind of opportunity that you have then, I would not have spent as much as I did. I spent a lot trying to understand the market and opted for the one that suitedmy kind of work, my kind of person and my interest. Because of that, I was involved in a lot of things. While at it, I made some mistakes and had some fantastic results. But in all of these, I learnt everything was part of business.

Mistake in business is not a crime. Making mistakes is one of the things that could help you in getting better in future. This is because you already have that experience and willbe wiser when you want to analyse its cause instead of blaming yourself or others. So, mistakes in business are not mistakes; they are platforms for linking your path with the success you deserve. This is because at the time you made the business decision that failed, you felt it was right. This continued until you realised that there was something more you needed to do and that you had to dispense with the previous approach or strategy and adopt another one. You will have clear understanding of this later in this book. When you talk about the strategies for identifying what you must do or planning your business, nothing stops either of them from being adopted or stagnant.

You can think of something now and move to something else later. So, creating a strategy is dependent on the analysis of your business environment. This will help you to make changes in future, should your strategy change from the decision you initially took. Judging from personal experience, you must ask yourself what you have been doing so far, what can help you build the future you need, which of your business decisions will be suitable for your kind of person and which of them will last longer.

If you are here and you have yet to start your own business or you do not have anything you are doing yet, this is an opportunity for you to sit down and plan this time very well. I believe by the time you finish reading this book and sign up for a one-on-one session with me, you will have more clarity on your choice and the running of your business professionally and profitably.

The fact that I understand figures as a professional

accountant gives me leverage to plan and analyse situations ahead of time. Whenever I am going in a wrong direction in business, my expertise helps me to quickly retrace my steps and make a recovery plan. However, for some business owners, this may be difficult to do. That is why some businesses go bankrupt and stop operations after five years. This happens because their owners do not understand the future or have a plan for it. They are in business with the mindset that business is all about struggles. All they see about business is money; they do not have the right approach to spending it. The word *hustle* is not far from their mouths. Remember, you are in business, not hustle.

If your mindset about business hinges on hustling, then you must change that NOW that you are reading this book. Business is business and you must treat it as one. When you do not understand that business has procedures, principles, processes, structures, regulations, ethics etc. that guide it, you will think that it is for survival. Business is beyond "I just want to do something" or "I just want to move on." It is beyond "just business." You have to be purposeful about it.

Early on, I mentioned what dragged me into having a side business. Having started a business with the impression that I needed more money, I realised what I needed was beyond money; I needed a structure that my future could rely on, a structure that would help me to stand outside business and a structure that would outlive me. These pushed me to where I am in my personal business today.

This necessity was more confirmed when I received a specific question on what God wanted me to project with my side business. I got to a level in my career where I felt that the income I earned from the side business was not equating its stress and that without the business, I could survive and carry on an assignment God gave me then: supporting women and youth. I was about to conclude on giving out items in my store as resources for the assignment when I heard the still voice in my mind, advising me to use the business to help others earn income. Immediately, I understood what God meant and changed my motive. I concluded that I did not have to shut down the business and that I could put a structure around the business and allow it to run on its own. During that period, I had the basic resources to proceed with the decision, so I went back to the drawing board, re-strategised and came back with a different purpose.

At present, I work at the executive level of a company as an employee, the CFO (Chief Financial Officer) specifically. Notwithstanding, I own my business in which I am the CEO (Chief Executive Officer). That is interesting, isn't it? For you, responsibilities in both capacities are seeming weight I put on myself. Amazingly enough, I do not see them as weight. This is because, after discovering my purpose in business, I was able to identify **the essential things that needed my involvement** (this required my attention) and **the routine ones around which I put a structure and engaged my team members**.

The foregoing lifted the burden from my neck and made the business independent. Over the years, we have been able to achieve much more than when I was doing it alone. As we continually ran it, it kept getting more people who had never done it before signed in and was recording huge income. It also provided income for members of my staff. In other words, it took them out of the unemployment circle and provided them with the real business world from which they could learn. If I had not redesigned my purpose, I would not have achieved these.

HOW I CHOSE MY TYPE OF BUSINESS

I naturally love to convert one naira to more of it. My lovefor moneymaking started when I was younger; it was like agame for me. This made me engage in sales of petty items, specifically food, when I was growing up. I also sold fruits in different seasons, confectionery of different kinds and fashion and domestic items after I got married. However, at a point, I realised I needed to create a niche for myself in the fashion industry to manage much better, especially when:

(a) It became increasingly difficult for me to manage all categories of business with my little funds. As a budding entrepreneur with limited resources, having too many things to do simultaneously became a challenge, especially when they started stretching my resources.

When you spread your investment across several niches to get "bits" of all instead of investing in a niche that will make you an authority in that line, you lose the opportunity to explore as expected and limit your growth. Please note that it is possible to divert to several niches if the resources are available. However, it is advisable to take it one step at a time so that you do not choke what you have grown to make you successful long before it starts yielding dividends.

(b) It became stressful, especially when I threw being an employee in the mix. There is no other thing that can create unnecessary stress than having too many irrelevant things to do at the same time. I call them irrelevant because it appears the control over the simultaneous management of all is lost. Engaging in activities that keep your time may project you as busy to the world. But as an entrepreneur, you need to be sure that all your tasks are relevant and have measurable results which are clear to understand. It is normal that works keep one busy and sometimes stressful. However, it is wrong if the accompanying stress is not equivalent to the required results.

(c) I began to aspire for growth. As I counted numbers of years in business, I realised that I needed more growth, not just in terms of fund I invested in the business or the huge stock I was buying, but, more importantly, in terms of the overall growth of business operations. I saw the need to push my brand out and be more visible. I began to see the need to position myself more on the business space and the need to do the right thing for business growth.

To resolve these aforementioned challenges and others not mentioned, I did the analyses of all the businesses I was doing at the time, using the level of risk that was involved in each of them and matching same with the resources required as well as my taste of risk for each of them. In subsequent chapters, you will glean from how I did these and how you can apply them to decision-making in your business.

After the analyses, I opted for shoes and wristwatches' distribution as my core business and other lines of business as support to the core. I even narrowed down the kind of shoes I would be dealing with as core to sneakers, leaving other kinds as support to the core. In consequence, my core products became my focuses for development. I built on the knowledge I had about them, increased my capacity and prioritised making sales from them unlike other few items.

For the sake of emphasis, I did the foregoing because I needed clarity. I designed a road map for my business growth, devised strategies on what I needed to do, identified resources and illustrated all through a financial plan. With these, I grew my business by 100% more than when I was doing it alone. I also noticed that my mind was at rest, thanks to the shared responsibilities among members of my team.

By implication, business owners should:

(a) Understand their priorities of doing business. They are not in business because people are doing it. They need to understand their *whys*.

(b) Understand the approach that best works for them in the operation of their businesses and give it their best. That others are doing it in a particular way does not mean it will work for you. You have to distinct yourself and create your unique identity.

(c)   Understand what business stands for. That is one of the things you will be getting from this book.

(d)   Be ready to grow their businesses. They need to keep feeding their businesses with ideas that will help them grow. They should always keep their minds open.

(e)   Know that they do not have to be involved in everything to make it in business. They can face particular lines of business and strategise how they will grow it to a self-sustaining level. However, after getting stabilised or established in a line, there is nothing wrong in creating another line of business. All they need is to plan ahead and equip themselves with enough resources to make it work. Yet, I suggest they stick to the growth of their original lines of business.

Other aspects of business are in this book to provide knowledge that will inspire you to have a good mindset towards your business and be determined to run it in a way that will make growth easy.

Chapter 2

MINDSET SHIFT – ENTREPRENEURIAL MINDSET

Entrepreneurial mindset refers to a specific state of mind which pushes human conduct towards entrepreneurial activities and outcomes. Individuals with entrepreneurial mindset are often drawn to opportunities, innovations and new value creation. Their characteristics include the ability to take calculated risks and the ability to accept the realities of change and uncertainty.

WHY ENTREPRENEURIAL MINDSET IS ESSENTIAL FOR BUSINESS

A. THINKING LIKE AN ENTREPRENEUR HELPS YOU RIGHT FROM THE OUTSET

Before you plan for your business, you must have figured out its details and shown the readiness to make money. With all these sorted out, it is normal to feel worried or anxious about your new venture. This is where you should begin to channel your inner entrepreneurial mindset into. Doing this will help you to think about what you are doing and why you are doing it. It will help you to know where you would like your business to lead you and what risks you are willing to take to succeed. If you know the answers to these questions, you will be ready to tackle all the challenges your new business throws at you.

B. IT HELPS YOU IN OTHER AREAS OF YOUR LIFE

Being willing to take risks and accept failure is a unique skill that is relevant in the business world. Incorporating an entrepreneurial mindset into your everyday life will help you to minimise the risk of failure and rejection in your life. It will also help you to keep moving forward even when things are difficult. Besides, being able to plan and foresee potential problems (a key part of an entrepreneurial mindset) will help you to live a more organised, less stressful life. In consequence, this will help you to run your business better.

C. IT ENCOURAGES CREATIVITY

That you start a business and things are going well does not mean there will not be challenges. To fix them, you need to be innovative and show willingness to take risks. Doing this requires that you should not always fall back on the simplest or safest way of fixing them. This is where critical thinking comes in. It is vital to the success of every business and enables you to come up with creative solutions to challenges, even if it means doing more work in the process.

D. PEOPLE TRUST OTHERS WHO SEEM TO KNOW WHAT THEY ARE DOING

The mantra "Fake it till you make it" is true in business. If you do your best to think, feel and act like an entrepreneur, people will treat you like one. By channelling your entrepreneurial mindset into business, you will be able to make new contacts with ease.

E. IT ENABLES YOU TO TAKE HEALTHY BREAKS

Work but do not overstress yourself. Rest is vital to your productivity as an entrepreneur. Successful entrepreneurs know that staying focused entirely on business is a sure-fire way of burning out. Go on international trips. Relax and visit new destinations. You will be surprised at the ideas and inspiration you get by experiencing new cultures. If you think like an entrepreneur, you will understand that taking regular breaks will benefit your business in the long run and that you need not feel guilty for indulging yourself with it occasionally.

TRAITS OF PEOPLE WITH ENTREPRENEURIAL MINDSET

If you have an entrepreneurial mindset, you can be an agent of change without even starting a company. Training yourself to have this mindset can make you more successful, regardless of what you do or where you work. Here are a few characteristics of a person with an entrepreneurial mindset.

A. CREATIVE THINKING

Challenging conventional thinking is a key trait of people with an entrepreneurial mindset. They see a world full of problems and constantly analyse it to find a more creative, simpler or more effective way to go about doing something.

B. TAKING ACTION

Those with the entrepreneurial mindset do not only see problems and think of solutions; they are also driven to bring those solutions to reality.

C. LISTENING

Egos destroy the best ideas. Those with an entrepreneurial mindset are focused on finding the best solutions, not having "their" ideas right. They are eager for input, actively gathering information and feedback and ready to iterate processes as long as they solve problems in the most effective way.

D. SEEING THE BIG PICTURE

Those with an entrepreneurial mindset think about things in a bigger picture context. They are focused on accomplishing the task at hand and are willing to consider all areas that may influence their success. Besides identifying the best solution to a particular problem, they ask themselves the time it will take, the amount it will cost, what it will create, what expertise it will need and what hurdles they will clear to get it done.

E. LEARNING FROM EXPERIENCE

Everyone fails. It is how people deal with failure that separates them from others. Those with an entrepreneurial mindset learn from failure. They understand that trial and error can be a powerful learning process.

F. IMPACT MAKING

At the end of the day, people with an entrepreneurial mindset want to make a difference. They can use that mindset to be an agent of change in a large company, in government, within a startup or small business or even as a university student.

You do not have to be born with an entrepreneurial mindset. All you need to do is to create time for this mindset to develop. The truth is that having it is worth your while, as this way of thinking will lead you to success.

WAYS TO DEVELOP ENTREPRENEURIAL MINDSET

Not every person is a born entrepreneur, but there are ways to teach yourself entrepreneurship, develop many of the entrepreneurial traits and embrace the mindset of the world's most successful leaders and innovators. Here are five ways to develop your talent and mindset in a way that will move you a step closer to becoming the entrepreneur that you want to be.

A. IMPROVEMENT

Successful entrepreneurs never think that they know it all. They are curious, eager to learn, motivated to improve their skills and never stop trying to become better at what they do and who they are. They believe that they should grow as professionals and aim to improve their skill set.

B. ACCEPTANCE

Successful entrepreneurs carefully choose their emotional battles and avoid stressing themselves about things that they cannot change. This is a feeling of liberation, which can help every person to concentrate on important things they can do something about, not on the things they cannot control. Successful people look for the opportunities in problems, not the opposite.

C. STAYING IN THE NOW

Successful entrepreneurs are never obsessed with their past mistakes; they learn from the past and move on. They concentrate on their present, trying to do their best. They understand that their future depends on their present, not their past.

D. VALUING NETWORK

Successful entrepreneurs work hard to build strong network

and support system and value all their connections. They are ready to expand their networks and strengthen their connections with other people who can inspire, motivate, advise and mentor them and vice versa.

E. CELEBRATING OTHERS' SUCCESS

Successful entrepreneurs help other people to achieve their dreams and goals. They are happy to see them succeed, given their understanding of entrepreneurship as being all about achieving something that can be beneficial for everyone, not just for one person.

MINDSET TO GET RID OF AS YOU DO BUSINESS IN YOUR LOCALITY

MINDSET 1: THIS IS NIGERIA. NOTHING WORKS HERE *(This can be about the locality of readers as well).*

Instead of having this mindset, say this to yourself: "Yes, this is Nigeria and a lot of things work here. The fact that we live in a developing country creates more opportunities for you. The truth is that there are lots of potential in this country, one of which you are. What sets you apart from those who think otherwise is your ability to identify the kind of problems or issues you can solve and create a niche around them. Develop the niche and see yourself adding value to yourself and your business.

Even in existing businesses, there are still a lot of gaps that have yet to be bridged. Yours is to identify those gaps, find how you can fit in and create solutions. This is called problem-solving. It gives value to the people who will be buying things from you. You may not necessarily go the way people go to solve the same problem. The decision on the approach you adopt to solve any problem in business depends on your risk level. Despite all, things still work in Nigeria or wherever your locality is, depending on the way you approach them.

MINDSET 2: I AM A HUSTLER. ANYTHING GOES.

You are in business to build wealth and enhance future growth, not to hustle. You are in business for others to benefit from in future. So, when you have a mindset that you are a hustler, you will do what is not in line with appropriate regulatory thoughts, standards, structures etc. With this approach, you may not achieve anything in business. As a business owner who wants to get the best out of your business or the people who engage with you - government, investors- you must be sure that you do your business in a way that will give value to others.

MINDSET 3: EAT ALL YOU CAN. NOBODY SEES YOU.

"Some people in business feel that I am the owner of my business. If I spend the whole or some of my capital on personal affairs, it does not concern anybody. If I take anything from the business, nobody is watching me."

You must change that mindset because, either directly or indirectly, someone is watching you. You will soon know this when you need something from them. For instance, if you have never considered paying taxes in your business and you think you can get off scot-free, you will get to a level in your business where you need a tax clearance to settle some things that have to do with items of benefits for your business.

At this juncture, you will discover how difficult it is for your business to operate. Since you do not have it and it is not something you are prepared for, there is no way you can enjoy the attendant benefits having it has. That said, what differentiates a successful business owner from the rest of the pack is their preparation ahead of opportunities; they are proactive. That is why they look beyond now and prepare themselves ahead of time.

MINDSET 4: MY BUSINESS IS MY PROPERTY. I CAN DO AS I LIKE WITH IT.

Your business is not your property. It becomes a public property the moment it becomes a business. This is because, going forward, you will engage some people in your business if you want growth, particularly stakeholders who are interested in your business.

MINDSET 5: ENTREPRENEURSHIP IS FREEDOM

This is a scam. As an entrepreneur, you have more to do to achieve your goals. That you own a business does not make you independent.

MINDSET 6: NOBODY SEES MY ACCOUNT; IT IS A WASTED EFFORT AND RESOURCE.

This speaks about keeping accounting records for your business. See more details on this in the latter part of this book.

Chapter 3

YOUR BUSINESS ENVIRONMENT SIMPLIFIED

If asked what an environment is, we will most likely mention everything that makes humans exist. That is the genesis of the definition of environment in the context of business. Just as the environment in which humans exist, business environment is dynamic. As a business owner, you need to do a continuous analysis and strategic planning of your business to ensure that it keeps its relevance. In this digital age, it is no longer enough to enter the market or start a business. You must consider how you intend to survive in such market. This means that if you are willing to survive, you must adjust your plans in a timely manner to any changes. In other words, you need to adapt to the business environment as soon as possible. And you can only adapt to the business environment you understand.

My aim here is not to provide any technical theories that

surround business environment as a topic, but to draw your attention to what you need to look out for to ensure that your business grows. In this chapter, you will learn a few concepts and factors that will make you understand this.

Business environment can be described as factors that have direct and indirect contributions to business operations. They are important factors that go a long way in defining how your business should carry out its operation daily.

External business environment includes social, economic, demographic, political and legal, global, competitive and technological sectors. Business owners need to have a good understanding of how these external factors of business environment change and their impact on their businesses.

Where there is a very strong and active **economy**, the rate of employment will reduce and the income level of individuals will increase. With this, it is most likely that business owners prepare business plans with a level of certainty of the conditions used for that purpose. It, therefore, means that the economy of the country or state in which you operate your business is a valid factor to constantly review.

In most cases, what applies in one place (country, state or city) may not be visible in another place. Your work is to confirm that your kind of business suits the economy of the country you intend to operate or operate from. This is what a lot of businesses that copy what they see working in businesses in other locations fail to understand. When their plan does not work out as expected, they become frustrated.

It is important to note that the revolution that is happening in the world of technology today is already uniting the world and businesses can now operate in an economy other than the one it operates from. You, therefore, cannot afford to limit your opportunity to your place of operation if your intending idea or current business does not fit into where it is at present. Be ready to analyse the implication of the economic activities that suit your business and plan your strategy in line with what suits your business most.

Government intervention on business, laws and regulations that bind businesses locally and globally and political stability are factors that contribute to the political environment of your business. For example, some months ago, in Nigeria, there was a ban on the importation of some items and the opening of land borders. This was done to encourage local producers of such items to increase their business activities and make them more efficient. However, this single act from the government of Nigeria generated a lot of responses from different business owners. It resulted in a complete shutdown of some businesses and the diversion into other businesses for those who acted fast, thereby expanding their scope of local production.

As a business owner, you need to follow the move in the political environment of your business and act swiftly should any situation happen. In whatever sector of business you operate, understand the type of political matters that could affect you and constantly review how you need to respond should the risk increase.

Studying people's key statistics or simply put, **demographics** is vital to many business decisions. Today, businesses need to deal with the distinctive interests of different generations. Each generation has a unique thing it prefers in products and services and that means businesses must adopt different marketing strategies for each category. You cannot sell a product meant for old people to the youth in their 20s. Your efforts in trying to sell have failed from the start. So, it is important that you analyse the value your product is offering and the problem it is trying to solve as well as the right category of people it is meant for. It is only when we get this right that we can plan marketing strategy right.

In my journey as a fashion items' distributor, there were times

I dealt more in selling wedding rings and outfits. Although I was selling a number of them to the people I knew closely and those who were referred to me, I knew something was missing. I could feel that I was not growing and there was no way I could continuously adopt that approach that I would not eventually die.

At some point, I added several other items to it in the hope that customers would have a wider range of products to choose from. This would make me know that if aproduct was not selling, another one would. While that sounded as a good strategy, my mistake at the time wasthat I did not analyse the demography of my customers, an activity that would have helped me to understand the exact category I should focus on. Remember, while at it, I was an employee, one who had used her access to funds gathered from her salary and ended up suffering due to wrong approach.

In fact, because I did not do this analysis well, I made a huge mistake by attracting wrong people when I was placing advertisement on my Facebook page to create audience and target for my business. I lost several leads because I was not prepared for the market I had outside Nigeria and because I did not understand the best logistics that suited them. Looking back today, especially now that Iam more informed,

I feel I made a costly mistake and learnt my lesson the hard way. That is why I am taking you through the processes involved with this book. I congratulate you for having a copy and reading it.

Competitive environment is another important area that businesses need to analyse and be more proactive in dealing with. In responding to this, business owners who desire growth and successes in their businesses need to maintain a balance between how to stay competitive and, at the same time, be profitable. The increasing rise in technological innovations, consumer expectation as well as foreign market openings have made competitive environment more aggressive. Business owners should ensure that they do not neglect the growth of their businesses, which can be measured from the profit businesses generate over time to the cost of responding intensely to market competition.

As good as promotional items are for businesses, you need to understand that your investment in them will speak positively to the bottom line of your business and will improve your financial position. You should not adopt too many strategies or less of them to manage this environment. What should be your driving factor is your perfect understanding of the kind of market your products or services operate in. If you operate in a free entry and exit type of market, it means that it costs nothing for any competitor to come in or out of the business. In fact, prices in this type of market are largely predictable because they are already saturated. So, if your strategy to stay competitive is to reduce your prices drastically, you might just be cheating your business.

Since your direct cost input is likely to be the same, your profit reduction may not be sustainable in the long run. In consequence, that may do more harm than good to your business. Discount, either product or cash-related, is not the only factor to manage competition in the market. You need to deal with how your value is perceived by your customers and find a way to distinguish yourself from others so that you can gain loyalty. So, you need to prioritise the understanding of your target and the creation of the right value that will meet their needs in your business. That you have a beautiful office or store and provide product or offer service does not mean you will get the right patronage if you fail to do this analysis.

Technological environment is another critical area today's business owners must not take for granted. It is now almost every day that business technology pushes businesses to evaluate their approach to providing their products or services to customers. For manufacturers, technology determines their production styles. The business technology mentioned here are digital tools such as computers, telecommunications and the Internet. The increasing expansion of the internet globally has forced many businesses that have been operating in the old- fashioned way (i.e. physically) to start going virtual (i.e. e- commerce). The benefit of this is that the usual limited market has now been opened globally and businesses can now penetrate and generate leads beyond the immediate environment they are geographically located in.

Customers do not have to live near your store before you deal greatly in business. They can access your products or services conveniently from where they are. However, the implication of this to businesses is that customers can now easily compare the features or benefits as well as the prices of your products or services with others' when making their buying decision. This means that business owners are now under more pressure toensure that they create a distinctive value that will open up more opportunities. This further means that the technology environment could have a direct impact on competitive environment.

It is, therefore, important that businesses that operate in today's world need to be very observant to understand trends that emerge daily, not just about the digital tools but also in the way the market uses them. For instance, I have always been operating my business online. I record more sales online than physically. However, when I restructured the business a few years ago, I made a 5-year business plan and financial plan. I did a few analyses and concluded on the type of products that I would be selling. I did these to have clarity on the exact products I would be selling. Instead of dealing with everything and having less control on my resources, I stood my ground on the approach I wanted and that helped me to create a niche for myself over time, planned the right human resources and located the exact type of online space where my customers were. One important lesson learnt from my actions is: that a lot of businesses massively flood social media daily does not mean they will generate their leads directly from there.

Since I restructured my business, I have been able to target and service my market better and understand the needs of my market. These are the key things every business owner needs to achieve. Whatever your business is, finding the right online space for your business to thrive is one area you should not ignore. This then means that you need to understand how this works, even if you are not the one who will be doing the task daily. You need to understand the basics of the market and allow a virtual assistant to take care of the routine exercise. You also need to understand the legal implications of the virtual projection of your products or services. This confirms that technological environment could also have impact on legal/political environment.

These factors affect business activities and the direct or indirect workings of your business. Overall, the factors mentioned above influence your business environment and situation.

Internal business environment is a factor that impacts the ways or methods of operation of an organisation and determines its success. Compared to external factors discussed earlier, internal factors fall within the control of the business. You may understand the potential threats and opportunities around your business but managing the strengths of your internal resources and approach to operation is very essential to the success of your business. You need to use internal environment as a tool for distinguishing and growing your business.

For businesses that already have employees and the ones that have to consider structures for growth that will make them have certain people to work with, managing them determines how successful your business will be. A lot of business owners have limited their business growth because they are scared to leave the affairs of their companies in the hands of strangers.

You have a fantastic business idea, but you fail to see the need for building the right team. This will continually limit or even make you lose ideas to another business that understands your weaknesses and can create a similar distinctive business to override yours. A lot of small business owners do not grow today because they fail to see possibilities of growth around their businesses. How can you be the manufacturer, marketer, customer service and logistics agent and accounting officer of your businessfor years and make exponential growth?

In this age of business, you still believe that there are business secrets you do not want to share with others despite being a hustler. Until you change this mindset, you will continue to experience marginal growth and you will think that is all that you can achieve. Break out and think beyond the corner you have boxed yourself to.

I understood this truth more when I considered that Rennyshouse might affect my main job. At this juncture, I was doing the side business all alone and had to let go of some juicy deals because of time factor. Some customers could not wait until I had time to confirm their products. The only people who understood me were those who were closely connected with me (family, friends etc.). That said, you need to break through the confines of targeting those who closely know you to experience a global growth.

It got to a point when I thought of quitting and concentrating on my career fully. But after receiving an inspiration from God in a weekly programme of my church on a Thursday evening, my thinking about quitting changed. The inspiration came as a thought, asking me whether stopping the business and giving out all my products would impact me greatly.

Thinking deeply about the fact that God can start with anyone all over again, I said NO. This led to the question about whether my response would be different if I considered the impact the business would make as an investment in other people's lives. Yet, my response to this question was a resounding NO. It was then I realised that God had been preparing me for a cause beyond me. Remember, my motive was to earn extra income from the side business. However, along the line, I felt that I was not getting much to justify my initial motive again. And with my experience in the business world, it is not wrong to change your strategy or business if that is the only option you have after a thorough analysis.

The inspiration birthed the strategy I adopted to restructure the business and engage competent hands. After I was through with restructuring, I identified individuals with the right qualifications needed to perform the task as expected and narrowed them down to OND, HND or BSc holders. This was done in line with my new motive, which was **adding value to individuals**.

Afterwards, I came up with this mission statement: **to ensure that the business adds value to fresh graduatesand serves as the bridge between the time they disengage from school and the time they get their ideal bigger jobs**. With this, I concluded that they would have the opportunity to create value for themselves in form of salary. I also created clear communication and made it a culture in the business that the essence of spreading our value and increasing our customer base is to ensure that customers who are interested in our products earn income from either the primary or secondary source. This and many other strategies were used to manage the team I engaged and it worked. I did not just add value to people. I did it in a less stressful manner and we grew massively.

What the foregoing means is that you should deploy one of the key approaches to managing your employees as an internal factor of your business; ensuring that you have a business culture, policies and procedures that guide your business and communicate them clearly to your team. You also need to continually involve them in decision-making and make them see WHY you do that. This makes them have a sense of belonging and act in the best interest of your business even when you are not there.

The role of leadership to business is considered an essential internal factor. This includes leadership style, approach to managing people and the business as a whole which, in turn, impacts the business culture. Most of the time, businesses prepare a formal structure with clear mission and vision statements. This is one essential exercise that can help you to have clarity and focus on the approaches to take in the business. Your leadership style, particularly, can impact how you value your employees and how you manage communication level between family and friends, thereby sending a negative or positive signal to your operation.

Organisational and functional procedures are key internal factors that businesses need to clearly identify and manage. You need to manage the business in a way that will send the right signals to your customers or clients. A simple disruption to your key tools such as the website for your e-commerce business could send a wrong signal to customers. You need to create a functioning approach to how you operate within the business such that it is easy to identify when there are issues and how to adopt the best approach to managing the business. In other words, there is need to create controls that will help you monitor the efficiency and effectiveness of operations between your identified and documented procedures.

WHY BUSINESS ENVIRONMENTS?

Based on the discussion so far, we can agree that business environment is the most essential aspect of any business. If a business owner, therefore, understands the continuous changes in the business environment, it will not only help the business to adapt to these changes but also use them as opportunities.

One thing to note is that your business environment could either make you see the threats or available opportunities for your business. So, it is important that business not only identifies and evaluates the environment but also reacts to these external forces. The importance of the business environment can be neatly understood if we consider the following facts:

A. YOU WILL SEE BUSINESS OPPORTUNITIES

It is not all changes that are negative. If you can take time to evaluate and analyse such changes, they can be the steppingstones to your business success. It is very important to continually and proactively identify changes and use same to solve problems of business in general. For example, my understanding of the need of severalemployees to have other sources of income in Nigeria and my experience as an employee trying to do same opened my eyes to the opportunities in the Rennyshouse's niche. That is why the business was able to increase its real customer base between 2019 and 2020 by selling online and targeting more of customers in this category who needed to solve supply matters in a timely manner.

B. IT ALSO HELPS IN IDENTIFYING USEFUL RESOURCES

Understanding your business environment in a more detailed manner will go a long way in picking useful resources meant for the business. Picking the right resources will help you to convert them into goods and services.

C. IT MANAGES CHANGES

You need to understand that business environment changes. These changes could be in the form of new government policies, technological changes, customers' requirements and emerging trends. If the business is aware of these regular changes, then it can bring about a response to deal with those changes. For example, when the Android OS market was booming and customers were opting for Android devices for their easy interface and apps, Nokia failed to cope with the change by not implementing Android OS on their devices. As a result, they lost tremendous market value.

D. IT HELPS IN PLANNING

This is another way of thinking of the importance of the business environment. Planning simply means what we will be doing in the foreseeable future. Where business environment shows a problem or an opportunity, the business needs to decide what plan it will come up with to take care of the future and solve the problem or maximise opportunities. After analysing the changes presented, business owners can incorporate their plans into their business operations to prevent the changes for a secure future.

E. IT HELPS IN BOOSTING PERFORMANCE

The identification and analysis of your business environment will not only deal with the changes presented but also flourish with them. Adjusting to external forces helps the business to improve its performance and survive in the market.

STAKEHOLDERS' EXPECTATION AND MANAGEMENT

It is important to discuss the concept of stakeholders and how they are vital to the success of your business. As business owners, you need to consider the analysis of these stakeholders and how best you need to respond to them toget the best out of your business.

Stakeholders are individuals and organisations that have interest in the strategy you make in your business. The term itself is used loosely to mean several things which are determined:

(a)   By how their interests are affected by what the organisation does. For example, they can be employees who need jobs or investors who need profits.

(b)   By how they have a legitimate claim to be considered by the management when decisions are made. For example, the management may want to consider the impact of the decision on future generations.

IMPORTANCE OF STAKEHOLDERS

Stakeholders are an important part of the ecosystem of the business. Stakeholders' engagement is a key principle in a sustainable business. For example, if a business does not ask its customers what they want, how can it expect to sell very much? If it does not engage with government, how can it expect to avoid unfavorable legislation?

STAKEHOLDERS' STRATEGIES AND THEIR PURPOSES

Literature on stakeholders seems to be on two different interpretations of a stakeholders' strategies. They are:

A. ENGAGEMENT STRATEGY

This states that the purpose of business strategy is to meet the requirements of stakeholders by delivering value to them. This fits into the ecological metaphor for business which states that a sustainable business is one that evolves to cope with its ecosystem and sustains that ecosystem.

B. MANIPULATIVE STRATEGY

This strategy projects stakeholders as either supporters to be enlisted or resisters to be overcome. The purpose of this stakeholders' strategy is to manipulate them and make the strategy successful.

CLASSIFICATIONS OF STAKEHOLDERS

(a) **Internal Stakeholders**: These include the management and employees.

(b) **Connected Stakeholders:** These are shareholders or investors, banks and other financiers, customers and suppliers.

(c) **External stakeholders:** These include governmental bodies and civil societies.

STAKEHOLDERS' ENGAGEMENT

This is the process by which an organisation involves the people who may be affected by its decisions or can influence the implementation of its decisions.

BENEFITS OF STAKEHOLDERS' ENGAGEMENT

A. ALIGNMENT OF BUSINESS AND ITS ECOSYSTEM

Understanding what customers, investors, partners and regulators want can help drive long-term sustainability and shareholders' value maximisation.

B. SUSTENANCE OF COMPETITIVE ADVANTAGE

Stakeholders can be an important source of information about changes in the business environment. These changes include changing tastes, technological changes or are about their own plans which can affect the business.

Chapter 4

KNOWING JUST THE RIGHT STRATEGY FOR YOU

The choice of strategy to use at any point in time is one decision that determines the growth of businesses. Before discussing strategy choices, you need to mention the strategy formulation processes. In formulating strategy, the three major activities required are strategic analysis, choices and implementation.

Analysis means that business owners should assess the current position their businesses are in and understand the expectations of the business stakeholders, as they are the ones in the position to judge the success of the strategy. The stakeholders in this sense are people or institutions that have an interest in the business strategy. We will treat the concept of stakeholders later in this book.

In performing this task, businesses should also identify the type of resources needed and the capabilities of their resources. In other words, they should be able to know the capacity they can take at the moment. You will not want to start a sales strategy to grow your business that will involve huge investment when you are not certain that the business has financial capabilities to sustain it or whether the impact will even grow the business as expected.

Sometimes, business owners operate from the point of blind faith. For instance, someone who wants to breed fishes should analyse the available resources and their capability to carry out the project. They need to understand the business environment in which this type of business operates to know how to identify the strategies to manage them. They also need to understand the interest of the stakeholders which, in this case, could be the customer, the feed vendor, the vendor for the pond (lease or build) etc.

These are the factors that will help to identify various strategic options that are available to take care of each of them and on which the business will make choices. That is why it is advised that you count your cost before you proceed with the execution of any project. The reason is to help the business avoid pitfalls during operation. A lot of businesses have experienced early death because this was taken for granted.

Strategic choices have to do with how to take a decisive position that will move the business forward. In doing this, the business must identify various strategic options available to explore in a situation. Take time to evaluate those options and eventually pick the most appealing. This exercise is done by considering each of the options in line with the company's vision, mission and value statements. It also needs to consider the viability of the option and availability of necessary resources. That an option appears good does not mean that it will be viable for your level of operation.

Another factor to consider when making business decisions is to check the most efficient option among the ones considered. What this means is that as a business owner, you need to have more than one option to choose in a particular situation and show readiness to analyse these options objectively, thereby helping the business to grow as expected. Where the selected choice fails, you will be confident that you have undergone the necessary processes in making the decision and can, therefore, win the trust of your stakeholders.

Strategic implementation is simply making your strategies happen and implementing them in your business. To get this done, you need to do a proper allocation of resources through budgeting. Budgeting will help you identify the need for resources to be allocated within what the business can generate.

Without proper planning of resources, which is clearly monitored in a *financial plan*, you may overlook the best approach to manage your resources and limit the growth the business can experience. The right leadership is also necessary during the implementation of your strategy. As a business owner, it is important that the approach implemented in carrying out your decision is strategic. You must be proactive or forward-thinking. This also means that you should look out for the same trait in the team you engage on your business. That is why you need to equip yourself with relevant training, read articles and attend seminars that relate to your business.

One other importance of appropriate strategic implementation is for business owners to perform appropriate target settings for their key performance indicators (KPIs). For a fashion business owner, your key performance indicator may be customers' happiness or satisfaction with your services. Your target could, therefore, be set on the number of positive feedback in a year. What it then means is that you need to set up controls to monitor your procedures. For the same example mentioned, you may have to include a trigger question or interview that will compel your customers to do a review of your services as part of your post service activities. Since you have a set target, you have to keep track of this by documenting it appropriately.

There are a few concepts of strategy that are important to all levels of business and, more especially, the potential of new startups. They are three strategy formulations which every business owner needs to know: intended strategy, emergent strategy and freewheeling opportunism.

Rational strategy is also known as rational approach or strategic planning approach. It is a typical planning process which is usually logical; a step-by-step approach used to carefully analyse circumstances, formulate strategies, choose the most appropriate option from and implement. Theoretically, this process includes:

A. MISSION AND OBJECTIVES

Businesses should set what their ultimate goals are and should give overall direction to the business - specific goals and targets. For example, the provision of world- class service by a business owner who deals in graphics.

B. POSITION AND APPRAISAL

Detailed analysis of current situation by examining internal and external factors affecting the business, resources and stakeholders. For example, a graphic business owner will have to analyse the services of its competitors, what more the customers expect and the resources available for the mission.

C. STRATEGIC OPTIONS

Suggesting suitable options the business could opt for to achieve the goals.

D. EVALUATION AND CHOICE

The company chooses the strategic plan that is best suitable for the circumstances.

E. IMPLEMENTATION

Putting the strategy into action and setting the plan in motion - organisational strategies

F. REVIEW AND CONTROL

Checking whether implemented strategies have helped

achieve the mission and objectives. If they have not, business owners should revise strategies.

A business that is willing to adopt this approach needs to have a well-trained professional to get things done. It is time-consuming and may not be the right strategy for a business environment propelled by uncertainty. For this approach to work, you need to have a level of certainty about factors that will be considered in the plan.

Emergent strategy unfolds as a result of circumstances rather than logical and formal planning. In this case, business owners develop and adopt strategies as circumstances occur. They are unplanned strategies arising from responses to unexpected opportunities and challenges. When this happens, a plan is first implemented and if it fails, another one is implemented. In other cases, it may mean that the business has a formal plan but wants to adjust this strategy to suit unexpected circumstances.

During the first wave of the global pandemic, a lot of businesses had to adjust their business plans to remain in business, using customers' engagement as their approach. Given the various policies made to curtail the spread of the virus, strategies for dealing with customers changed a great deal. With this approach, business owners need to be alert and dynamic to business strategy, as it helps to take care of the various limitations of the intended strategy approach. Nonetheless, it is quite challenging if the approach is adopted by not-so-smart business owners.

Another example is a honey processing company called PICKY (pseudonym); whose initial strategy was to sell honey for consumption. If the company's CEO discovers that there is an increasing market for the use of honey as a beauty product or a government policy or an act puts the beauty products' companies that use honey as a raw material for their products to promote healthy skin at a very attractive and premium position in the market, they need to analyse the cost benefit of this new development and ascertain that the company's position in the market is better. Going by emergent approach, PICKY may want to create a new line of products that will deal in beauty products or completely divert to the business.

The other strategy approach that is categorised as an entrepreneurial approach to business strategy is **freewheeling.** This is what most small businesses adopt to avoid any formal planning and take only opportunities that come their way. For example, in the fashion industry, where taste and development of patterns change fast, it may be difficult to adopt any formal planning, depending on the niche for such a fashion business. In that case, you have no option but to move in line with the most current wave of fashion taste.

Businesses that use this approach invest in ideas that take advantage of opportunities. However, for this type of approach, they may find it difficult to identify the key risk involved in implementing it, as that is not the focus area that is driving their decision. Also, for owners who intend to raise funds for their businesses, this strategy may be difficult to adopt, as most investors (including shareholders) or fund providers want to see the detailed approach of how they plan and execute their businesses.

It is important to note that there is no perfect or best approach to strategy. That is why you should identify what suits your business in terms of products/services, vision, business environments etc. and select the appropriate and efficient one to use. You must analyse the benefits of any of the approaches you intend to use along with their challenges and check whether you can manage them effectively. Remember, the approach you can clearly interpret and defend is most likely the best for you.

As a visionary or someone supporting the pursuit of a vision, you need to understand that your business approach to strategy does not have to be based on what other businesses are doing. However, it should be adopted based on what you see as appropriate and unique to your type of business.

STRATEGIC PLANNING FOR NOT-FOR-PROFIT ORGANISATIONS

Strategic planning can be challenging for not-for- profit organisations such as charities, schools, hospitals etc. This is because they have:

A. MULTIPLE OBJECTIVES

Unlike profit organisations, they do not work for profit. This causes conflicts in the achievement of their objectives.

B. MULTIPLE STAKEHOLDERS

With multiple stakeholders come conflicting demands. Each of them has their vested interests, doing all they can to protect them.

C. DIFFICULTY IN MEASURING QUALITATIVE OBJECTIVES

Due to the dearth of research tools, it is challenging to measure quality tools.

D. STAKEHOLDERS WITH EQUAL POWER

Unlike companies where shareholders have more power, there are multiple high-powered stakeholders here. For example, a school has parents, the government, local education authority etc. as its stakeholders.

E. NO PAYMENT FOR SERVICES

Users of these services are not necessarily paying for it. This is commonplace among learners and patients in public schools and hospitals funded by the government.

F. SET KPIs (KNOWLEDGE PERFORMANCE INDICATORS)

KPIs are set by the government to control and check whether the objectives are met. Since NFP (not-for-profit) organisations do not make profit and their successes or failures cannot be estimated, use the following approaches:

THE THREE E'S APPROACH

A. ECONOMY

This is the level of the input use and the economical use of its funds. For example, knowing whether or not the funds hospitals expend have increased or reduced.

B. EFFICIENCY

This deals with how well input is converted into output: efficient utilisation of input. It is about doing things right. For example, the cost per patient incurred in a hospital.

C. EFFECTIVENESS

The level of final output achieved. This is done by checking whether the ultimate goal of the organisation is met. For example, the total number of patients who recovered from sicknesses or reduction in mortality rate etc.

BUSINESS MODEL

This shows how your business defines, creates, delivers and captures value for, with and to its key stakeholders in a consistent and coherent manner. Moving forward, you need to know what value means.

(a) Value means benefit to the customers or users of your products. Without creating value, your business cannotexpect any value through sales.

(b) It means benefit to society. If your business provides no benefit to society or causes harm to society, it will be prohibited or banned and forced to stop operation.

(c) It means benefit to employees. Such benefit could be in the form of payment of salaries or wages, training, increasing capacity and security of the human resources in your business. These benefits are essential to keep good hands in your business.

Every employee wants to feel that your business can add value to them. To identify how much you can give as value to your employee, you need to understand what the labour market looks like for the level of the person you engage and check that with your business operation through your financial plan. The essence of the plan is to confirm that the business can conveniently make the payment.

(d) It also means financial returns to investors. For businesses that have investors or are willing to have, the value they can create for stakeholders is to make good

profit that will guarantee a good return for them. No investor wants to invest in anything that is not profitable or does not give value that is in line with their purpose of investment.

ACTIVITIES OF VALUE CREATION

These are the four core models of business:

A. VALUE DEFINITION

This is the establishment of the value your business seeks to create. To do this, you have to:

(i) Identify the stakeholders on whom the organisation impact.

(ii) Identify what is more important and what is less important.

(iii) Formulate a value proposition to them according to their requirements.

For instance, in the case of:

I. CUSTOMERS

Decide your target customers and the sort of benefits they will get from your products or services.

II. SOCIETY

Identify near neighbours and interested groups and establish a corporate social responsibility policy that will benefit them.

This is not the case for a very small business because CSR (corporate social responsibility) comes with a cost and the company may not have enough resources to work with. Whatever support given to society should serve as a benefit to such that is linked to business branding.

B. VALUE CREATION

This means the use of resources, supply-chain networks, processes and activities of the business to deliver value. The value you create relies on the output it generates, products or services you offer, jobs, happy or satisfied customers, better society and wealthier investors.

C. VALUE DELIVERY

This determines how value is received. This model refers to segments and channels. For example, several ways through which customers can receive the value your business creates depends on how you have segmented them and the channels you use for the distribution of your products or the delivery of your services, e.g. e-commerce, agents, own stores and so on.

D. VALUE CAPTURE

The management makes arrangements to ensure that the business maximises the financial value it creates. This may indicate the common management accounting technique of revenue and cost management. Your business should not just be selling value but creating a means to account for it. Many business owners believe that accounting or record keeping is meant for professionals alone, but this is not true for entrepreneurs. There must be a clear approach to capturing your operation. While Excel is okay for some businesses, there are different accounting software that make it efficient for small businesses to capture their value.

For you to experience necessary growth, I recommend SAGE Business Cloud Accounting software. We use this software at Rennyshouse and this makes it easy for us to account for every business operation and use report from it to make decisions.

LEVELS OF BUSINESS GOALS

There are several levels of objectives. These are:

A. FUNDAMENTAL GOALS AND OBJECTIVES

These are the people or groups who benefit from an organisation and the key things the organisation does to deliver value to them. For example, if there are benefits for investors, their fundamental goals will be financial.

B. SECONDARY OR ENABLING OBJECTIVES

These are the steps on the road to reaching fundamental goals. An instance is the sales target for a sales group of any organisation, which is an objective of that department. However, it is intended to play a part in achieving a financial objective.

VISION, MISSION AND VALUE (VMV)

A. VISION

(i) This is a statement of what the organisation hopes to achieve or become; and

(ii) It is a description of a future world.

B. MISSION

(i) A statement of what the organisation intends to do nowto realise its vision.

C. VALUE

(i) A moral direction of an organisation; and

(ii) The behaviour of an organisation and its staff members.

ROLES OF VISION, MISSION AND VALUE (VMV)

A. STARTING POINT FOR STRATEGY

Developing a strategy has to do with your business making progress in a way that is consistent with its values. Your business VMV may also be the expression of the goals of key stakeholders of your business.

B. GUIDE TO BUSINESS BEHAVIOUR

The values you identify with your business are in effect an ethical code for the business. You will support consistency in your business if you define the code of conduct that supports your operation and trains your representative (employee or outsource agent) in the business to behave accordingly.

This is also your business culture of values, beliefs and behaviour that define the nature of your business and should not be frequently changed. Once you define this culture, it becomes your brand and whoever encounters your business will remember it.

C. BENCHMARK FOR ASSESSING STRATEGIC OPTIONS

If you are faced with different strategic options to explore, it is ideal for you to check whether any of the strategies fit into your VMV. The strategy with the best fit will be the best one to adopt. This helps consistency in your operation as the business grows.

D. DEVICE FOR GAINING SUPPORT FOR BUSINESS

The intention of VMV is to be shared or published for the public to know what your business stands for. Some businesses use their websites to display this. Some include it in their business newsletters, while some include it in their business proposals for prospective customers or clients.

Whatever format you use to communicate your VMV, it is important that you use them to gain support from other stakeholders in the business. It is, therefore, not enough to write an attractive VMV of your business without its appropriate behaviour. This will only make your VMV useless. Though VMV can attract people and institutions to your business, it is your organisational behaviour that will keep them.

E. BASIS FOR KEY PERFORMANCE INDICATORS (KPIS)

You need to set KPIs for each of the commitment spelt out in your VMV. This will help to monitor the implementation of such commitment. If this is not done, it is easy for you to forget the content of your VMV and start acting in contrary to it.

Chapter 5

MANAGING BUSINESS ASSETSFOR GROWTH

Business assets are items of value that your business creates, owns or benefits from. Assets include your cash balances, customers, stocks, office equipment, intellectual properties etc.

One of the things that businesses require for growth is the adequate management of these assets. They are key items that give life to business. The same way you manage your health, knowing full well that all your body parts are integral to your living, is the same way assets are managed for business.

In business parlance, an asset is a resource of value that belongs to your business or you lease from another party that helps you run your business. These are tangible items such as petty cash and equipment or non-physical things such as brand, reputation and goodwill.

Assets, in accounting terms, are items that you can sell or convert to cash or use to produce value. For example, your inventory, bank balances, accounts receivable, prepaid expenses etc. Assets accounts are very important factor in your business' financial position. Depending on how you look at them, assets can fall into different categories. Generally, assets can be categorised into **natureand type**. Based on their convertibility to cash, you can classify them as either:

A. CURRENT ASSETS

These are assets with a short life span and that can easily be converted to cash.

B. FIXED ASSETS

These are intended for long-term use and are unlikely to be quickly converted to cash.

Another way of grouping business assets is according to their **physical characteristics**. Under this approach, you can distinguish between tangible assets (physical, material and financial resources of your business) and intangible assets (resources without material substance but with a clear business value. Business assets can also be labelled as either operational or non-operational based on their usage.

As good as assets are, their improper management may lead to the death of the business. This is a major challenge businesses are daily finding solutions to. For instance, stock (products meant for sales) should be managed in a way that it will provide optimum benefit to the business. Too much stock may tie down your cash, create financial risk and force you to sell at any amount, especially when the business is facing cash flow challenges.

On the other hand, too less of stock level could also mean that you are missing your target market share, especially when your loyal customers have to consult your competitors when you do not have the quantity they need from you. This is the same as other categories of assets.

No matter the level of your business, you need to recognise that your assets are important to your business and should be properly controlled. Even as a business owner, you are not expected to use your assets outside your business and when you do, they must be adequately recorded and stated that they are within a range of reasonable use. If you must take your stock, for instance, you need to properly account for it in your books as an owner's drawings. And if you intend to pay for it but have yet to, it should be recorded as receivables from you to thebusiness.

This is in line with the rule that the business is an entity on its own and should be separated from your personal life. You must treat your business as though it exists on its own. Just as a parent wants their baby to develop, business owners must ensure that they give their businesses the opportunity to grow by feeding them with the proper approaches and laid down principles that make business survive.

To create control around your assets, it is important to consider:

(i) Putting a structure around your business if you have yet to do so. Putting structure in this context means separating responsibility within your business by identifying the processes involved. Identify the current level of your business and where you will love to see the business in future. Have a clear understanding of the available resources and the growth plan in future.

Based on this ideal process, you need to identify the human resources required to get the work done and prepare the organisational structure of your business. Do these even when you have yet to engage people there. Creating such a structure has a way of sending growth signal to your subconscious mind and encouraging you to do the right thing to achieve it.

Having done that, you may not necessarily have to put individuals in all these positions at once. However, based on the size of the business and needs of your staff members, you may identify the ones that can be merged. This is the starting point for creating job descriptions that will be used for announcing the needs of staff members.

(ii) Engaging the right skilled team in your business. A lot of business owners engage their family members or friends in their businesses. Some even engage them based on pity, not on merit or competency. As good as this can be, ensure you are professional or disciplined enough to extend your business culture to such individuals to make them respect the controls set around your business. Be ready to train and support them if they are incompetent. If you cannot control them, it means that you are putting a high risk of survival on your business. Therefore, set a trigger time to when you need to back out of such engagement.

I remember when I first put a structure around Rennyshouse Services, I intended to engage three people to start up with me. Before I employed them, I had spelt out my expectations of their competence and the task I would want them to do. I also identified the target I would evaluate each of them on in the first three months of their engagement.

Armed with this understanding, I publicised the vacant positions, shortlisted participants, conducted interviews, engaged and trained them before they commenced work. A few weeks into their resumption, one of my customers mentioned that I help someone close to her get a job.

Considering the biased mind I had for the person of my customer and her request, I failed to make the person undergo the processes others went through before I engaged her. Even though I communicated the same target, I realised that she was more interested in the salary than the job, as she could not meet it. But because I had set a triggered timing of three months, it was easy for me to terminate her engagement.

(iii) Creating a business culture and value and communicating them to your team in an efficient and effective manner. You will put your business at risk of asset mismanagement if you fail to define the culture and value your business rests on. Your team must understand these before they can appreciate what the business has to offer. In the absence of clear communication, they may not understand how essential it is to manage your assets even in your absence.

A. STOCK

Stock management is vital to business growth. Stock is the heart of any business. Whether your business is into production, marketing and distribution or services, there is an element of stock that is required. Particularly, production and distribution require more direct stock that is meant for items to be sold than the ones for operations. However, a service providing company will only look at stock basically from items meant for its operation. Whichever it is, stock management is a key factor of business sustainability.

In this part of the world, we cherish family and friends so much that we find it difficult to separate social matters from business matters, thereby making our businesses open for easy access to all. Sometimes, you see family or friends picking your stock items for free and ignore them or fail to take a proper record of the value of the items taken. If this continues, there is no way such business will grow.

Stock management is the function of understanding the stock mix of your business and the different demands on the stock. Demands are influenced by both external and internal factors and are balanced by the creation of purchase order requests to keep supplies at a reasonable or prescribed level. It is important for every other business enterprise.

One of the key tasks of stock control is stock count. It is important that you do this to ensure that your stock items are properly monitored. For businesses that deal primarily in merchandise of products, stock is central to their existence. As a business owner, its effective control will help you gain overall control of your business operation and will guarantee your sustainability. Other ways of achieving control over your stock include:

I. CONSIDERATION OF SEGREGATION OF DUTIES

Where the scale of your business can allow such, you can consider sharing duties among different staff members such that there is distinct approval or check on stock items' movement.

II. REVIEW OF STOCK COUNT

Apart from the person that will conduct the stock count, there should be another person/agent that will support in doing an independent review/check to be sure everything is done accordingly. This is not to say that your team cannot be trusted; it is to create certainty around your business.

III. APPROPRIATE STOCK TAGGING ANDKEEPING

For businesses that deal in a variety of stocks, it is ideal if you tag and arrange your stock appropriately. In case you need support to get this done, it is worth the effort. Your stock items are to be easily identified physically or virtually.

B. PEOPLE

For any business to experience growth, it needs committed people. They can either be directly employed or outsourced to the business. People management, also known as human resources management, is the function of recruiting the right personnel, managing them on the job for optimal result and continuously providing support and direction for their development as they help the business to grow.

Getting the most out of people in your business means your business has consistent policies and practices in place to provide people who work with you with appropriate training and development. People, in this sense, are employees and you need to understand that they are involved as "partners" in the business. Your staff members are called partners because they speak the same language as you. So, your key task, as the owner of the business or manager who engages in the business, is to see how you deal with people in your business in a way that gets the best out of them.

When engaging people in your business, make sure you follow

appropriate recruitment procedures that will help you engage the best hands, not just anybody to fill your office space. Your kind of business will determine the skills you need from the person or people you are engaging. This should be appropriately checked during the recruitment process. Depending on the scope of your business and the level of the person you want to engage, you may want to do a background check.

Apart from the company that professionally does background job, another way to know the person you are about to bring to your business is to check their social media platforms. Their online presence will give you a clue of their personality and this will help you raise a few more checks to confirm the value they are bringing to your business and sometimes how you manage them.

Recruiting the best hands is not the final stage in people management. You have to constantly train them on skills, policies, procedures, values and behaviour that you need from them to achieve success in your business. Therefore, do not assume they have all it takes to grow your business because they meet your criteria. Training and developmentare the sole of people management. Some of the skills that you need to effectively manage people who support you and your business are:

I. EMOTIONAL INTELLIGENCE

This is the ability to manage yourself to impact others. It involves the activities you engage in to understand, use and manage your own emotions in a positive manner and to relieve stress, empathise with others, communicate effectively with your team, defeat challenges and manage conflicts. This skill is required for every aspect of your business that has to do with people.

As a visionary of your business, it is possible for people you engage on your business not to have a full understanding of your vision. Sometimes, it is possible to get frustrated if they are working outside what your business stands for or are taking too long to understand what you are communicating. You, therefore, need to master the skills of emotional intelligence to deal with everyone appropriately. Emotional intelligence skill, as a subject, is quite broad and cannot be fully treated in this book. However, it is important that you take time to study and acquire the skill so as to manage people in your business better. Enrol in a course that relates with the subject if you know that you are still lagging in this important aspect of leadership. Beyond the knowledge acquired, be ready to operate your business with this understanding, as it is integral to the appropriate utilisation of other skills.

Among others, emotional intelligence will help you achieve:

II. PATIENCE

This is one of the skills that everyone thinks they are in control of until they are at the peak of a situation where things get tough. Although a lot of people are naturally inclined to be more patient than others, that does not mean they should not develop the skill. Being patient will help you keep your head up in the face of challenging situations. When you find yourself in situations that can make you lose your cool, try the following exercises:

- **CLOSING YOUR EYES**

Take deep breaths through your nose and out through your mouth. Slowly count 10 in your head (One-Mississippi, Two-Mississippi works well here). This simple technique will help you stay patient and calm during the most trying circumstances.

- **TRUST**

Leading others is all about trust. You need to trust that the people you engage in your business have its best interest at heart. You need to trust that they can work and achieve your business goals with you.

Agree with yourself that with or without your supervision, they will be able to achieve this task. One of the rules of business is that "You can't do it all." The earlier you understand this fact, the better it is for your business. This is because, at some point in the growth phase of your business, you need to delegate. This requires that you trust your team and yourself if you want to be an effective team lead.

III. ABILITY TO RELATE

This is exhibited through the following qualities:

- **EMPATHY**

This has to do with your ability to understand and share the feelings of others. In other words, it means showing compassion. For instance, if any member of your team is going through a critical situation such as loss of a close family member or someone close is ill, it will be great if you can show some level of empathy for their situation/challenges. You have to consider this as a necessity because if you are the one in that kind of situation, you will appreciate being treated kindly. That is what it means to show empathy; to understand that some situations may rob someone of their productivity at a particular period. It is putting yourself in others' shoes.

To get the best out of them in such situations, you have to ease their work or help them stay focused till the situations get resolved.

- **OPEN MIND**

This is not talking about having your way or the best way; it is the ability to leave all opinions open until they are considered good for your business. Yes, you may be the one who owns an idea as a business owner. But to get the best out of your team, you need to be open to them and allow them to air their opinions, as they may be speaking from what the core market projects at the time and which may be beneficial to your business. So, to have an open mind, you have to conclude that you may sometimes not have the best answer to situations.

It is not enough to have an open mind. You also need to let your team know that you have it. This will help to create trust and respect between you and the team. By having an open mind, your team will have a positive feeling that their views, suggestions and feedback count and are valuable to your business. This will also make your team view you as approachable and easy to work with.

- **HONESTY**

If you intend to build a powerful team that trusts you and one another, honesty is one key factor you need to display. As a business owner, you need to treat your team the sameway you wish to be treated. They must see you saying the truth in good and bad situations. It may also require you relating with them truthfully even when it is not in your best interest. By doing this, you are teaching them that dealing honestly with you is normal.

This skill will help them to improve on their work and

approach to dealing with one another. It will also enhance a healthy working environment and improve productivity. The implication on this will be more reflected in their output and will play a huge role in the growth of your business.

- **POSITIVITY**

If you want your team to exhibit positivity, you must display same. This may mean facing tough situations, projects or challenges without uttering negative words or complaining. When they see you display this attitude, they will be encouraged to do same.

When you are in the face of tough work, accept the situation as reality and show excitement in getting it solved in a unique way and within a deadline. Shifting your viewpoint from the issue and not seeing it as an obstacle help you train the mind of your team and motivate them to do the same.

- **GOOD COMMUNICATION**

This involves a wide range of skills, four of which are listening skill, speaking skill, writing skill and reading skill. The first two mentioned here are very essential for people management. Good communication will give you the ability to get along with your team, to persuade them, to get them to listen to your views and to get clarity on what you always say. Getting clarity always is essential in people management to save the time spent in achieving a task. Your team members must clearly understand what you are saying or the idea or suggestion you are projecting. This will help them to respond or act appropriately and to get it right the first time.

IV. CUSTOMER

Another key asset to any business are the customers. You must have heard of the saying "Customers are kings."

Customers are the life wire of any business and that is the reason why any business owner will do all that is necessary to manage their interests.

The reality is that the growth rate of your customer is directly related to the growth of your business. The process your business uses in managing the relationship between your business and your team is called customer management. Your vision and goals are expected to form one of the bases for identifying customer management strategies. This is one of the reasons why you see companies creating departments specifically for customer services.

It is important that you take customer management very seriously at whatever level your business operates. Beyond setting goals, you need to create a culture and system to manage your customers. It should be integral to the daily operation of your business. You should also have controls deliberately infused in your process to check whether your system is working. For instance, when I restructured Rennyshouse and engaged staff members to work with me, they became the company's ambassadors and related directly with customers. Even people who knew me closely and wanted to deal with my business were directed to them. The essence is to maintain consistency and avoid dealings that are inconsistent with laid down culture for the business. We have a WhatsApp group where almost all our wholesalers and distributors are added to receive communications and updates about our business activities. Although, I am in the group, I do not usually engage customers. I allow my team to do that.

Occasionally, I train them on how to manage the business or send greetings or articles that will be beneficial to them. During the activity, I indicate my name and my position within the business. The reason I do that is to keep my channel open for customers to connect if they have any issue with any of our approaches and want me to deal with it.

There are instances when I receive such messages, I deal with them by creating highlights around them in the group. This depends on the gravity of the issues and after making enquiries. The reason I choose that approach is to enlighten other customers who may be having same issues but do not have the courage to talk. This approach helps me build customer loyalty to our brand and manage their continuous patronage. It is important to adopt strategies that will help you manage your customers in a way that will earn you mutual respect for your business.

Moreover, your developed customer relationship management is the one that should help you turn leads into customers and sustain them in your business. Most of today's customers want to have personalised experiences with your business. They all want to be treated as being important. This then means that your business needs to analyse and understand what turns your customers on and what their interests and expectations are. Having known these, you, therefore, need to deliver on your expectations beyond what your competitors will do.

The five key stages for customer relationship management are;

- Reaching a potential customer;
- Customer acquisition;
- Conversion;

- Customer retention; and
- Customer loyalty.

V. MONEY (CASHFLOW MANAGEMENT)

Your business money is another key asset of your business which requires effective management. A business that lacks appropriate fund management may not survive even when it operates with clear and beautiful strategies. The first step to manage the financial aspect of your business is to prepare a financial plan based on your strategies and manage the progress through the analysis of the results they give you. Chapter 6 gives detailed approach to getting this done.

Financial management includes bookkeeping, preparation of your financial statements and financial opportunities of your business. All these are the bedrocks for achieving your business goals and making right decisions.

As a business owner, you need to acquire the skill if you do not have it. This is because it does not augur well for you to be complaining about how your capital disappears. I am not saying there is no spirituality to life, but most of the business failures you see all around are the results of the business owners' refusal to be aware of or disregard.

On a lighter note, even when there are spiritual matters, you should be able to explain how capital vanishes from your business if you undergo the process of your business as expected. In other words, you have a role to play in managing your business funds. When you engage people in your business, this understanding has to be part of what you imbibe in them so that they know they are fully involved in the process of financial management for your business. The person who makes sales will know the importance of documenting record of sales.

The overall objective of managing your money is to ensure that profit is maximised. That is one of the things that existing or potential investors in your business growth will be interested in. Financial management is important at all stages of business. So, you need to ensure that this is analysed and well interpreted to determine your next strategy for growth.

Chapter 6

WHAT I NEED TO KNOW ABOUT BUSINESS PLAN DEVELOPMENT

Winston Churchill said, "He who fails to plan is planning to fail." Business planning is one area where most businesses are still lagging. It is not different from the way you do proper planning if you need a good building or want to win a football match. You may not get the best from your business if you operate with no plan.

I am aware a lot of businesses feel that the process is too technical or tedious. However, they should know that failing in a business endeavour is more disastrous. A business plan is an accumulation of information and decisions made during the planning process of a business. It helps you articulate how you are going to seize and execute your great ideas. All business enterprises contain risks.

Preparing a business plan, therefore, identifies areas of risk and minimises the problems which will inevitably arise. A business plan is a written tool that helps increase the odds of success. The preparation of a business plan is an essential step in the starting and financing of any enterprise. It is written before a business owner starts a business or when an update of some areas of the business are required.

A business plan is:

- A document which spells out the goals and objectives of a business and clearly outlines how and when they will be achieved.
- A structured guideline to achieve a business goal.
- A road map to owning and operating a business.
- A proposal that describes a business opportunity to financing agencies or investors. A discussion paper for possible funding assistance from banks and investors.
- A detailed action programme outlining every conceivable aspect of the proposed business venture.
- It is a record of the entrepreneurs' intentions, the historic background of the project, their reasons for undertaking it and the different stages of development.
- A medium for informing prospective investors and bankers and also providing a yardstick against which both the management and investors will monitor the success achieved.

OBJECTIVES OF BUSINESS PLANNING

One can list many things to answer the million-dollar question: why a business plan? The following reasons elaborate why a business owner needs a business plan.

A business owner needs a business plan because:

(a) They need to map the future and establish business milestones.

(b) The challenges a business start-up come across are partly predictable. Being proactive and systematic is one way of facing the business start-up challenges. Preparing business plan is being systematic and proactive.

(c) They need to support and secure the required business start-up finance. Accessing various sources of financing starts from planning the business in SME startup loop. Here, an entrepreneur calculates the investment and finance requirement which enable them to know how much finance the business start-up requires in detail. A business plan helps to communicate this clearly to interested parties, especially investors and creditors.

(d) Business management competencies and start-up needs to be developed and readied. While planning the business in SME, the entrepreneur learns, improves and enhances business management competencies. Starting and running the business requires business management competencies.

(e) They need to manage business finance and capital. Sometimes, potential entrepreneurs mix up business finance with household finance. Business financial management essentially starts from treating business as a separate entity and keeping accurate records of accounts. Business planning gives the entrepreneur the awareness and strategies to manage finance and cash-flows, especially the working capital management.

(f) They need to grow steadily and scale up their business. Planning equips the entrepreneur to respond to changes and prepare for future success. It helps to identify and put in place precautionary measures that guarantee business success. It provides a basis for comparing company's actual results with planned results to investigate variances and take corrective measures.

HOW TO WRITE A BUSINESS PLAN

Provided below is a step-by-step guide on how to write your business plan from scratch even if you have never done it before. You can follow the process to prepare your own business plan and should be ready for the benefits that lie ahead of your business. It is advisable that all business owners have copies of the business plan for their businesses as opportunities in business sometimes do not announce themselves. Nevertheless, the rule is that anentrepreneur must be prepared ahead of growth opportunities.

Below is a typical business plan template you can adopt if you want to write it from scratch. Business plan content includes:

Executive Summary

1. *Introduction*
2. *The Product/Service*
3. *Industry and Market Analysis*
4. *Competition*
5. *SWOT Analysis*
6. *Operations Plan*
7. *Marketing Plan*
8. *Management*
9. *Financial Plan*
10. *Appendices*

Executive Summary

This is a summary (or a snapshot) of all the contents of the plan. It should be written in such a way that anyone reading it will see the core or essence of the plan. Executive Summary should cover every section from Introduction to Milestones.

1. Introduction Overview

Describe the business. State the stage of the business:

- *Research and development stage*
- *Market entry stage or*
- *Growth stage*

If already existing [growth stage], describe the current operations. State the progress made so far and what spurred you to take the next steps for which you are writing this business plan.

Vision Statement

This is a statement of what you want your company to become eventually, e.g., one of the top 5 in the industry, the most preferred for the service etc. You may state the time frame for attaining the vision. The vision must be inspiring to drive you to higher performance in the business.

Mission Statement

This is simply the statement of the purpose for which the business is set up and is trying to achieve; its reason for existing that indicates the problem the company's product will solve and the market niche.

Objectives

This is a statement of what you want to achieve with the businessover a defined period. It could be to:

1. Establish your product/service in the market,
2. Grow the business to a specific size.
3. Increase market share.
4. Increase profitability to a certain level.
5. Be a preferred brand.

Most importantly, your business objectives must be SMART:

Specific – Target a specific area for improvement or initiation.

Measurable – Quantify or at least suggest an indicator of progress.

Attainable – Specify who will do it.

Realistic – State what results can realistically be achieved givenavailable resources.

Time bound – Specify when the result(s) will be achieved.

Value Proposition

This is a promise of value to be delivered and acknowledged. It is what gives the target market an expectation of what benefits will be delivered and experienced from the product or service. It could be:

- Reduction in time
- Reduction in cost
- Enhancement of health
- Enhancement of efficiency in the customers' business or life etc.

2. Product/Service

Describe the product and/or service you are producing/offering or you will produce/offer to deliver the value proposed to customers. Include illustrations if necessary.

3. Industry and Market Analysis

- State the industry or the sector of the economy (health, agriculture, construction, manufacturing etc.) in which your business is playing.

- State the key features or peculiarities of the industry that make it viable or demonstrate growth potential.
- State the actions of government that support the growth of the industry.
- State the market you intend to serve.
- State the major players in the industry.
- State the size of the market (volume and value where possible).
- State the segments of the market – the different customer groups.
- State the specific group your product or service is meant for.
- State the potential for growth in the market.

4. Competition

- State your major (direct and indirect) competitors.
- Describe their product and service offers.
- State their competitive advantages or disadvantages.
- The customer segments they are focusing on.
- State the probability of new entrants.
- State the potential new competitors/market entrants.

- State whether the barriers they must overcome to enter the marketare high or low.
- State whether the cost is high or low for a customer to switch tocompetitors.
- State how you can make or achieve customer loyalty – making sure your customers will always prefer your products or services.

5. SWOT Analysis

- State your areas of strengths – skills/expertise, financial resources and unique selling point.
- State any existing patents, intellectual property, partnerships, collaborations and technical support you currently have or will soon secure and how they contribute to your strength.
- State any awards and recognitions achieved that can make your brand stronger.
- State weaknesses internally and even externally such as new untested products, weak brand, low level of adoption by target market etc.
- State the opportunities in the business environment that will assist the performance and growth of your business. Consider the political, economic, social, technological,

legal/regulatory and physical environmental factors (PESTLE) in your community, country, region or continent that may influence your business.

- State the threats, challenges and risk that you have to deal with(also consider PESTLE).
- State how you will enhance your strength and use it for competitive advantage.
- State how you can reduce your weaknesses.
- State how you can exploit the opportunities.
- State how you can reduce the threats, risk and challenges.

Strength	Weaknesses
Opportunities	Threats

6. Operations Plan

- State the patents and permits/licences you require to operate.
- State material resources (such as raw materials, physical assets, human resources and other input) and how you obtain them – by direct purchase, by suppliers, by buying agents, outsourcing, etc. and include the equipment needed to manufacture the products or offer the services.
- State other key resources (including intangibles like certification or new knowledge) you require.
- Describe how you will deliver the product or service to the customer (from production point to consumption point).
- State your suppliers and your expected method of relationship with them as well as your key distributors and/or agents (if any).

7. Marketing Plan

- State how you will make customers aware of your products or services. Be as specific as possible as you choose any of these options: digital, social media, TV, radio, newsprint etc.

- State how you will promote your products or services. Is it through trade fairs, TV talk shows and appearances, radio talk shows, focus meetings or strategic presentations?
- Describe the pricing strategy for your products/services and the assumptions you have made.
- Will there be any incentives that will make them switch from current providers or buy the products/services anew – discounts, credit facilities. Where possible, describe the effect of the incentives on your cash flow and profitability.
- State how you ensure that credit customers (if any) will pay.
- State the channels by which you will get the services to the customers. Is it through e-market place (on the Internet or any other electronic means), department stores/supermarkets, distributors, wholesalers or sales agents?

8. Management

Functions

- State and describe the functions you need to perform to run the business: production/inventory management, admin/facility management, human resources, finance/accounts, marketing/sales and other functions.

Qualifications/Expertise

- State briefly the qualification and expertise of staff required to perform the functions.
- State the calibre of staff members who will be (or are currently) responsible for functions such as production manager, personnel manager, accountant and marketing manager.
- State your roles and responsibilities in the business.

Organisational Structure

- Design this to show the coordination and relationship lines between and within the functions.

9. Financial Plan

Key Assumptions – on cost elements, current and future costing, financing options and revenues projections. Remember that it is prudent to underestimate your revenue and anticipate more in costs.

Cost Estimations & Projections

Cost of Facilities and Operations

- List the required facilities and corresponding costs to determine total cost and include assumptions on currency of purchase (whether they are locally available or need to be imported).
- Give cost breakdown for producing products or offering services – both direct and indirect – cost of raw materials and other input, repairs and maintenance, testing/quality assurance etc.
- Provide the estimates and projections of cost of running the business for 3 years – wages and salaries, capacity building, branding and advertising, packaging, administration, logistics, professional services, licenses etc.

Financing

State how you will finance the cost: with your savings/personal funds (equity), grants, business proceeds (equity), credit from suppliers (debt) or borrowing (debt), raising additional capital via the stock market or other forms like venture capital, private equity etc.

- Describe proportions if you are considering a combination of sources.
- State exactly how you will use the money.

- State how you will repay the debt.

Revenue Projections

- State the products and services from which you will derive revenue

   - your revenue streams.
- State the way you will price them.
- State the estimated volumes of products and services to be sold for 3 years – Year 1, Year 2 and Year 3.
- Determine the revenue projections for the 3 years.

Financial projections on the financial statements (For support to prepare financial plan, you can send a mail to peakpointschoolofbizandmgt@gmail.com).

- Determine the profit and loss projections for 3 years.
- Determine cash flow projections for 3 years.
- Determine balance sheet projections for 3 years.

Milestones and AttachmentsMilestones

State what you need to achieve each quarter for the next 2 years and the amount required to achieve each of them.

- Include milestones of output – products, solutions,

clients, patents, coverage areas etc.

- Indicate number of staff members – full-time and/or part-time.
- Include expansion/growth milestones that can be tracked perquarter.
- Avoid bogus, exaggerate or unattainable milestones.

10. Appendices
- Place additional charts, graphs and images here to support yourbusiness plan.

Chapter 7

PUTTING STRUCTURES INPLACE

Business structure describes how your business organisation functions. The intention of a business owner on how the business will provide its goods or services as well as how they intend to manage the control in the business will determine the best structure to put in place. Business owners need to register any structure they prefer accordingly with the legal body of the jurisdiction of intending place the business will be operating from.

TYPES OF BUSINESS STRUCTURE BYLEGAL COMPOSITION

The most common types of business entities include sole proprietorships, partnerships, limited liability companies, corporations and cooperatives. Here is more about each type of legal structures.

A. SOLE PROPRIETORSHIP

It is the simplest form of business entity. With this structure, the responsibility of the business profits and debts lies with one person. So, in a situation where you, as a business owner, want to be your own boss and do not intend to own a physical storefront, this type of legal structure will help you to be in perfect control. One of the main features of sole proprietorship is that, as the owner of the business, this structure does not separate or protect you from any liability that the business may have on its assets in future. This is a big issue, considering the possibility of having a legal filing that poses a liability or loss in the business in future. In other words, if the business cannot fulfil its expected obligation, a lien could be placed on your personal assets.

Some benefits of sole proprietorships include:

I. EASY SETUP

A sole proprietorship is the simplest legal structure to set up. Since your business is owned by you alone, there is very little paperwork you can do, as there are no partners or executive board members you are answerable to.

II. LOW COST

The cost of maintaining legal structure of sole proprietorship is very minimal, depending on your country. However, in most cases, the major cost is getting the certificate of registration or license and ensuring that business taxes are paid.

III. TAX DEDUCTION

Since you and your business are a single entity, you may be eligible for certain business tax deductions e.g., PAYE (pay as you earn).

IV. EASY EXIT

Just as it is easy to form proprietorship so it is to exit. Being a single owner, you can dissolve your business at anytime with no formal paperwork required.

B. PARTNERSHIP

This entity is owned by two or more individuals. There are two types: a general partnership (where all is shared equally) and a limited partnership (where only one partner has control of its operation, while the other person (or persons) contribute(s) to and receive(s) part of the profits).

Partnerships carry a dual status as a sole proprietorship or limited liability partnership (LLP), depending on the entity's funding and liability structure. If your intention is to go into business with a friend, business partner or a family member, you can consider this legal structure as appropriate. This type of business allows you to share profit or loss and make decision together within the structure. However, it is important to note that you will be responsible for any decision made by you and your partner. The cost of managing partnership is higher than sole proprietorship but fairly low.

The benefits of partnership include:

I. EASY FORMATION

Like a sole proprietorship, there is little paperwork to file.

II. GROWTH POTENTIAL

You are more likely to obtain a business loan when there is more than one owner. It is not that it is impossible when you are one, but it broadens the opportunity when you are more than one.

C. LIMITED LIABILITY COMPANY

A limited liability company (LLC) is a hybrid structure that allows owners, partners or shareholders to limit their personal liabilities while enjoying the tax and flexibility benefits of a partnership. Under an LLC, members are shielded from personal liability for the debts of the business if it cannot be proven that they act in an illegal, unethical or irresponsible manner in carrying out the activities of the business. The cost of registering this is actual high. Although small businesses can be LLCs, some large businesses choose this legal structure.

D. CORPORATION

The law regards a corporation as an entity which is separate from its owners. In other words, it has its own legal rights and is independent of its owners – it can sue, be sued, own and sell property and sell the rights of ownership in the form of stocks. The benefits of this structure include:

I. LIMITED LIABILITY

Stockholders are not personally liable for claims against your corporation; they are only liable for their personal investments.

II. CONTINUITY

Corporations are not affected by death or the transfer of shares by its owners. Your business continues to operate indefinitely, which is preferred by investors, creditors and consumers.

III. CAPITAL

It is much easier to raise large amounts of capital from multiple investors when your business is incorporated.

E. COOPERATIVE

A cooperative (co-op) is owned by the same people it serves. Its offerings benefit the company's members. Also called user-owners, it involves people who vote on the organisation's mission and direction and share profits. Benefits that cooperatives offer include:

I. LOWER TAXES
Like an LLC, a cooperative does not tax its members on their income.

II. INCREASED FUNDING

Cooperatives may be eligible for federal grants that help them get started.

III. DISCOUNTS AND BETTER SERVICE

Cooperatives can leverage their business sizes, thus obtaining discounts on products and services for their members.

For new businesses that could fall into two or more of these categories, it is not always easy to decide which structure to choose. You need to consider your startup's financial needs, risk and ability to grow. It can be difficult to switch your legal structure after you have registered your business. So, give it a careful analysis at the early stages of forming your business.

ORGANISATIONAL STRUCTURE

Your business is an organisation that operates outside your personal life. Your business structure, in this context, is the system that explains how your business activities operate to achieve your business goals. The activities mentioned here are the policies, cultures, roles and responsibilities embedded in your business. The structures indicate who does what on your business and the expectation you have identified from such activities that will help you achieve your goals. It also defines how reporting should be channelled.

Smaller and home-based businesses typically do not use organisational structures because business owners usually are responsible for completing the majority of business functions. Larger businesses, on the other hand, use organisational structures to effectively manage business functions and employees. This suggests that the type of organisational structure to use always depends on the company's size and operations.

Even when your business operates on a small scale, your strategy should include an expansion plan that will explain your growth level. Therefore, you may want to keep an ideal organisational structure and fill people with the functions as the business grows, depending on your business long-term plan. No matter how simple it is, your business needs a structure which will define how the organisation should be structured.

Although the structure only deals with the owner (and co-owners), the description may also include outsourced work together with their expertise and qualifications. All these will add credibility when introducing your business to prospective customers/clients.

Having identified the processes involved in the building of organisational structures and the people that will perform their functions, you should think of all the people involved in your business and the relationships among them and draw an organisational chart.

BENEFITS OF ORGANISATIONAL STRUCTURE

A few universal benefits exist from the structures. They are:

I. STREAMLINED BUSINESS OPERATIONS

Organisational structures can help companies streamline business operations. Business owners, directors and managers are responsible for organising business functions into departments that can complete various business processes. Doing this ensures that business operations are completed effectively and efficiently. In the end, companies save money by reducing the number of similar business functions completed by multiple departments.

II. IMPROVED DECISION-MAKING

Companies can use organisational structures to improve their business decision-making processes. Business decisions often relate to the amount of information business owners, directors or managers gather within period. Organisational structures can be designed to promote the flow of information from frontline operations to managers responsible for making business decisions. Executive level management can use organisational structure channels for sending information to managers or employees responsible for completing business functions.

III. OPERATION OF MULTIPLE LOCATIONS

As small businesses continue to grow and expand, they may open multiple locations in local, regional or domestic economic markets. Organisational structures help business owners create a management chain to ensure all business locations operate according to the company's standard procedures. Business owners rely on organisational structures because the owner may not be able to visit each location as expected.

IV. IMPROVED EMPLOYEE'S PERFORMANCE

Organisational structures often outline employees' tasks and the manager who is responsible for overseeing each employee. Employees may undergo a training period during which they learn the company's organisational structure. This process informs employees which managers can take specific decisions or where they need to send information for approval. Organisational structures also can be created with some flexibility to add new departments or employees so as not to burden one manager in the company.

V. FOCUS ON CUSTOMER SERVICE AND SALES

Companies using a well-defined organisational structure

should be able to spend more time focusing on customer service rather than correcting operational issues. Improved customer service helps companies answer consumers' inquiries or questions regarding goods or services. Companies may also focus on increasing sales revenues and profits from business operations by meeting consumer needs and wants.

Chapter 8

SEEING YOUR NEXT 5 YEARS' PROFIT TODAY

A goal is a result which you or your business plans to accomplish, while strategies are various methods adopted to achieve the goal. Goals can be achieved in the long- or short-term, depending on the strategies that you develop and use in achieving them. As you adopt any strategy around your business, it is important that you set a plan around their financial implications. A business without appropriate financial plans may end up crashing even when they seem to be adopting fantastic strategies.

The main reason why you are in business is to make profit. How you channel this profit might be different from one business to another, depending on your core vision, mission or goals. To achieve your business goals, you may have considered different strategy options and may be tempted to explore one because it appears to be dominating, especially when it is channelled into the promotion of your brand.

You must be careful about what only decorates your business but does not speak to why you are in business, which has been established as profitability. I have seen new startups that are more concerned about the physical appearances of their stores or brands instead of the delivery of their products or services.

While business branding is very fantastic, you should know your limit per time, depending on the level you are on your strategy roadmap. I have also seen businesses that do not have a clear view of the number of resources they need and the quality of the resources end up having so many staff members beyond what their business requires. Some SME owners even consider it a thing of pride to claim that they have XYZ number of staff members under their control, not until reality dawns on them and they are forced to speak out for support. Some even refuse to get such support because they feel, out of pride, that they can put everything under control by themselves. In the end, they frustrate their businesses to death.

In business, you cannot afford to keep yourself in unnecessary frustration because you refuse to do the right thing. Most times, what you need is the right information and the readiness to apply it, not magic. That you have the right skills to do what your clients want but without the adoption of the right approach is not a guarantee that you will get it right in business.

You appear alien in your business the moment you do not learn business languages. For instance, there are exceptional fashion designers who have never experienced growth beyond where they started from. They have the same stores or frequently change them with the same capacity. They use the same machines or add a few to their machines once in 5 years. Amazingly enough, they believe that is the best their businesses can offer.

On the other hand, another person who understands how to play the game of business in the same industry and who started at the same level will experience exponential growth because they follow due process to achieve the result. They are strictly business-oriented and enjoy being like that.

The difference between the two groups is that one leaves their businesses to chance and sometimes do not even have the right skill on how to do a proper costing. They only see direct cost and forget the indirect cost. Everything they know about their businesses is only in the head. They have no documentation and that makes it difficult to analyse their performances and what they need to do to increase their business worth.

Anything that does not challenge you is bound not to give you anything extraordinary. While others take specific and controlled approach to business, do not leave anything to chance. If events beyond their control happen in their businesses, they quickly get back to the drawing board to plan a recovery approach.

It is, therefore, important to quantify whatever strategy you plan to adopt in your business. If you have more than one option, check the best by comparing some qualitative measures, prepare financial plan for each of them and check the one that gives best result to your business financial position.

Some business owners believe that they do not need any form of financial plan until their businesses get to a level. This is a big myth targeted to bar you from achieving growth in your business. Even as an individual, you need a financial plan. That is to tell you that your business plan starts from the period ahead of starting the business. If you have started without this key task, you must consider starting NOW and measure your growth alongside this.

Most times, what limits us is clarity on what we conceive as idea and how it will materialise. A financial plan is designed to help you put all necessary facts and figure together and present it in a financial statement format for you to see how they are speaking into your business. In other words, you will see, most importantly, your profit and lost statements, cash flow statements and, where necessary, your financial position statements for the period you intend to check.

In summary, to start your financial plan, you need to:

A. UNDERSTAND YOUR VISION

You need to understand what you stand for, why you are in business, who your audience is and why you intend to serve them. We have treated vision, mission and value in another part of this book. You may want to read them again. However, for the purpose of this session, the starting point of any business should be a well-defined vision.

B. SET THE GOALS

The next thing is to set SMART goals and objectives. These are the results you use to achieve your visions. SMART is an acronym for Specific, Measurable, Achicvablc, Relevant and Time-oriented. Whatever goal you are setting must achieve these qualities.

C. BREAK YOUR GOALS DOWN INTO SMALLER TASKS

You have to further expand the goals and break them down into periodic tasks that will make you achieve the goals. These are called strategies. You are not going anywhere if you only set goals without the strategies that will make you implement them. Goal settings are not done for formality's sake. That is the essence of SMART qualities that must be present in your goals and can make your task preparation/scheduling easy.

D. IDENTIFY THE RESOURCES TO ACHIEVE YOUR GOALS

After identifying the task, you will obviously need certain resources to get them done. You need to list these items out. So, if your goal is to hit 50% more of your sales in the previous year, you have to create additional channels for sales and target a particular group and create some promotional items or digital products that are attractive to them. All these point to resources you will need in the

process of getting the task done. You need to identify all of them.

E. CREATE CONDITIONS

Given that your financial plan speaks to the future, which may not be certain now outside the environmental trend that you can use to project it, it is necessary that you analyse your business environment and create the conditions that your business plan will be based on such that it will be easy for you to check the gap between your actual plan and future plan.

F. QUANTIFY AND FORECAST

The last task is to quantify each of these resources and use it to prepare your financial plan.

BENEFITS OF CREATING FINANCIAL PLAN

My intention is to shift your focus from the tasks involved in preparing a financial plan and see the benefits therein.

This will help you to put in place the necessary procedures that will help you and your business grow. In this section, I will highlight a few benefits you will enjoy if you adopt the use of financial plan in your business.

- **IT HELPS YOU SEE THE VALUE CREATED AT A GLANCE**

We have already established the fact that businesses exist to create values. Sometimes, we may underestimate or overestimate these values if we do not analyse them in a manner that shows how it feels to have a business. One thing I know about financial plan is that, sometimes, the idea or strategy might be fantastic until you start seeing the reality in your financial plan. Immediately, you will be informed about whether or not you need to adjust any of the conditions you initially considered. Therefore, it is a wise and progressive decision to always consider all your strategies through the analysis of the financial plan.

- **IT HELPS TO IDENTIFY WHERE YOU NEED FINANCIAL SUPPORT**

When financial plan is prepared, the resultant cash flow trend will indicate how healthy your cash flow will be if you must consider the strategy you are proposing. In a situation where the strategy is quite viable but there is a period of the year when there is fund shortage, that will tell you whether you need to get financial support or rearrange the timing of your operation within the cash that the business can provide.

Without such financial plan, you may have to blindly consider the strategy and get your business stretched beyond normal in such period. In most cases, it may be difficult to be effectively managed.

- **IT PREPARES YOU AHEAD OF POTENTIAL INVESTORS**

Most investors are comfortable with investing in your business when they can visibly see how the funds they are investing in your business will be utilised and their results. That is why loan or grant requires that you submit a business plan. If you see the content of the business plan template provided in this book, you will observe that financial plan is included. Some investors are more particular about financial plan because that will fulfil their main objective of investment, which is to maximise profit or wealth.

- **IT POSITIONS YOU BETTER IN YOUR INDUSTRY**

Being able to proactively prepare your financial plan indicates that you know what you are doing. This will put you in check and distinguish you in your industry, even if everybody does the same business that you do. Having a financial plan shows that you understand how business operates and you are being proactive with your moves. If any reasonable project is available for players in your industry, you are much prepared for such and you will be able to respond appropriately.

Sometimes, the opportunity that will launch our growth does not announce itself ahead, but it is only an individual who has prepared ahead who fits in easily. So, when we preach that you need to run your business as a business, we do it to get you always prepared for every opportunity. Apart from the one you will enjoy within the resources you are operating with, you will also positionyourself for potential ones.

Chapter 9

WHY YOU SHOULD KEEP APROPER RECORD

A lot of small-scale businesses have yet to master the culture of record-keeping. This does not exclude some well-established and large-scale businesses. Record keeping contains various activities channelled to ensure that the operation of a business is documented for future use and key business decision-making. A lot of stakeholders are interested in the reliability of the approach businesses use in keeping record, as this record forms the basis of a financial statement that records the summary of the results of all business activities and the performance of the company.

OBJECTIVES/IMPORTANCE OF RECORD KEEPING AND BUSINESS PERFORMANCE

A good accounting system should give an accurate and comprehensive result of operations, which allow quick comparison between current and previous data, offer the financial statements to be used by prospective creditors, bankers and management, facilitate filing reports and tax returns to government regulatory agencies, tax collecting, disclose record keeping error, waste, theft and employees' misconduct.

It is asserted that the success of a business depends, to a reasonable extent, on the accuracy of record keeping. Accounting systems grant a basis of information to SME owners and managers operating in any industry for the usein measurement of financial performance.

Good record keeping enables business firms to plan properly and curtail misappropriations of resources. It is also observed that keeping good financial records can positively influence management decisions of business owners or managers. The most important information to an entrepreneur comes from the accounting information, which is akin to the score card of an enterprise. They are indicators of growth potentials, earning ability, liquidity and stability.

An efficient and effective record keeping is important to any organisation, as it affords a measurement and communication mechanism which can help in improving the quality of decisions and actions which affect the way the scarce resources of an organisation are utilised. The difference in financial performance of SMEs can, to areasonable extent, be explained by the level of record-keeping.

Objectives of record keeping include:

- Provision of accurate picture of operating results.
- Preparation of actual records with budgeted figures.
- Comparison of operating results of years of operations.
- Preparation of financial position useful to business owners, creditors, prospective investors and bankers.
- Filing of tax returns to various tax offices and usage by other government agencies.
- Revelation of employee's fraud, theft, waste and errors.
- Preservation of vital accounting records and destruction of obsolete records; and
- Support of loan applications to financial institutions.

Benefits of record keeping are as follows:

- Prevention of business failure.
- Sound financial planning and control.
- Some help in decision-making.
- Business survival and success; and
- Revelation of the background picture which helps organisational change.

Record keeping shows the health status of a business. These are some of the reasons why small business should keep records:

- Record keeping helps entrepreneurs to fulfill their tax obligations.
- It helps entrepreneurs know how their businesses are performing.
- It provides entrepreneurs with facts for good business decisions.

The roles of accounting information in the improvement of the performance of SMEs include:

A. USAGE AS A CONTROL TOOL

It helps to detect fraud carried out by employees of an organisation.

B. MAINTENANCE OF ACCOUNTABILITY

It helps in maintaining accountability over the assets of a company like cash, stock of goods, furniture and fittings and other movable assets. Proper accounting system should be set up to minimise opportunities for misappropriation and theft of assets.

C. PREVENTION OF LOSS THROUGH CREDIT TRANSACTIONS

It helps in credit transactions. Credits are offered today by SMEs to stay afloat. Improper record keeping can lead to loss of income, especially when credit transactions are not well monitored.

D. SOLUTION TO TAXATION ISSUES

It helps in solving taxation issues. There are various forms of taxes paid to the government e.g., Pay as You Earn (PAYE), withholding taxes, value added tax (VAT) etc. Proper record keeping is germane to determining accurate taxes to be paid by a firm, thereby avoiding over-taxation or under payment of taxes as the case may be.

E. PROFIT DETECTION

It helps in knowing whether a business owner makes profit. The primary motive of running a business is to make profit. It may be difficult to find out whether a firm is making profit or not without adequate record keeping.

The use of accounting information could be linked to the success or failure of an entrepreneur. There is a strong relationship between business performance and the level of training in the business management, especially in business finance record keeping.

Knowledge and skills in bookkeeping are essential, as they have positive impact on the sustainability and growth of SMEs. The concept of performance is used to determine the success of a business entity whether small or big.

The International Accounting Standard Board (IASB) conceptual framework specifies that profit is frequently used as a measure of performance. Business performance can be measured in term of business size, employment capacity, turnover, capital base and profitability.

WHY SOME SMEs DO NOT PREPARE RECORD OR HAVE POOR RECORD KEEPING

Despite the importance of record keeping in monitoring of the businesses, some SMEs do not give needed attention to record keeping. Some of the reasons attributed to lack of record keeping include time, cost, lack of knowledge by business owners and employment of unskilled accounting staff members. It is observed that some business owners have the tendency to rely on their memories rather than keeping proper books of accounts, while some business owners believe that keeping proper business records will expose them to pay more tax. It is also observed that most SME owners recruit unskilled account clerks who cannot prepare accurate financial statements. This has stagnated the growth of some small businesses and made their owners completely unaware of how their businesses are performing. If care is not taken, some eventually fold up.

Some of the excuses entrepreneurs give for not keeping accounting records include:

A. TIME CONSUMPTION
A lot of SMEs are so interested in a daily turnover of money that they feel that setting another time for bookkeeping is

time-wasting. It is important that you know that bookkeeping is more beneficial to you as a business owner. It helps you to analyse issues more efficiently and helps your business to gain clarity. The little time spent on this gives value that is much more beneficial.

B. EXPENSIVENESS

The good thing is that, depending on your business, there are accounting packages that help you perform the task with less stress and help you to have important books of record and financial statements even if you are not a professional accountant. This software helps to generate necessary reports that can be useful in making informed decisions on your business inasmuch as you follow through the guidance on how to use them effectively. When you consider the benefits of keeping proper books of record, the cost is very minimal and should have been included in your business plan if you have done the same.

C. TECHNICALITY

As I mentioned above, there are software that help perform this task. As a business owner, if you are not the one to do the daily uploads of your activities, it will be ideal that you understand how the information thereinworks and how it can be useful for your business. Taking acourse on accounting for non-accountants is one way to understand this in a very simple language you can understand.

Most of the agents who install accounting software also provide necessary skills and their technical know-how. You may have to sign up for such training for yourself and your team that will be using it. The truth is that there is no right investment that is done in your business that will not yield multiple results.

D. ADDITIONAL STAFF MEMBERS

You can adopt and use the accounting software by yourself if the scale of your business is still low and you cannot hire staff members.

E. EXPOSURE OF EMPLOYEES TO FINANCIAL POSITION

Some believe that keeping such record will disclose their financial strength to their employees. It is important to note that we need to carry our employees along in what we are doing so that they have a sense of belonging and will be able to perform their duties. However, you may want to set limit to the extent of their access to your system. Despite this, their exposure on the job will define the experience that they can count.

F. PAYMENT OF MORE TAXES

Sometimes, doing the right bookkeeping will help you to know that you do not have any tax to pay. With that, you can do your tax filling without fear. Running a business that ensures compliance to law and regulations is veryimportant so that you do not face unnecessary issues with the authority in future.

G. NON-KEEPING OF ACCOUNTING RECORDS

Some business owners, especially SME owners, disregard the importance of record keeping, thereby claiming that there is no need to keep accounting records.

H. DIFFICULTY IN MAINTAINING AN ACCOUNTING SYSTEM

It is observed that most owners or managers in Nigeria see their businesses as their private affairs and, therefore, disregard their accountability and transparency to anybody.

Chapter 10

WHAT WOULD YOU DO DIFFERENTLY?

Having understood various business concepts and reasons for taking your business more seriously, you should take necessary steps for the growth of your business. Do not just read this book for reading's sake. Implement its contents.

Topics treated in this book are not exclusive to all your business needs. However, they form the basic and important aspects that all levels of businesses need to understand to become better. You, therefore, need to take a decision and charge yourself to do your business in a different manner. For each of the sections, identify key areas you would love to imprint on your business and set goals around it. These goals do not have to be achieved within a short time. You can plan it for the future, but it is important you consider taking a step.

Be open to accessing information continuously. If you desire growth, you need to make personal development dear to your heart. Nobody grows without information. Make yourself available for learning. However, the type of course to sign up for must be relevant to what you will need to implement your strategies.

You also should not keep quiet on things that are disturbing you in your business. Learn to reach out. Peak Point School of Business and Management is your plug on matters relating to business and management.

BENEFITS OF LEARNING/STUDYING BUSINESS MANAGEMENT

Learn about the benefits of studying business management if you want to become an effective leader. You can grow your small business by investing more time in learning about business management techniques. However, you first need to understand basic business management concepts. If you own and operate your own business, you are already engaged in the practice of business management.

From making plans to assigning tasks, you are always in control of your company. Of course, strong organisational skills are a necessity, but you also need to display consistency in every aspect of managing your business. Remember that your ultimate goal is to make constant improvement to ensure that your business continues to thrive. The following five benefits of studying business management strategies can help you build a profitable business.

A. MORE KNOWLEDGE ABOUT BUSINESS

The main benefits of studying business management are that the skills help business owners comprehend known methods of operating their businesses. Small business owners particularly benefit from the advantages of studying business management. The importance of studying management is that the course helps entrepreneurs who do not have enough experience in handling various types of challenges.

A few benefits of studying business management include learning how to create a business plan and master your own accountancy, how to negotiate business deals and how to improve your analytical skills. The importance of studying business management includes improving your ability to attain success. You also have the capability of making decisions regarding your expenditures. The main advantages of studying business management focus on a general improvement of your qualifications as the owner and manager of your company or corporation.

B. LEARNING PERSONNEL MANAGEMENT

Owning a business entails a vast array of talents. One of the advantages of studying business management is that you learn how to manage employees, including supervisors and managers. Studying management techniques centerson your ability to become a better communicator and listener. Therefore, when employees have complaints about their jobs or duties, it is helpful to know how to address their problems in a professional manner.

You learn how to encourage workers to accomplish their goals and how to discern the types of abilities inherent in different employees. Another benefit is that you knowwho to hire as your managers. Plus, you acquire knowledge regarding how to train upper management personnel within the finance and general business operation fields.

C. LEARNING COMMUNICATIONTECHNIQUES

If you own a small business, you must have a gift for communication. Even though you might not be born with the gift of the gab, you can still learn how to communicate when you study business management. Any valid business management programme automatically teaches you how to become a better communicator. After all, communication is the heartbeat of your business.

You must communicate with your employees, clients and colleagues and may even need to know how to express your thoughts to fierce competitors. Business management classes teach you how to perform quality research and write complex business plans. You can then present your projects to an audience.

Communication involves more than talking and writing; body language is an important aspect of good communication too. Learning how to communicate via your body is one of the significant benefits of studying business management. Basically, you learn how to think, speak and act in a leadership role.

C. DEVELOPING A SUPERIOR SENSE OF SELF-CONFIDENCE

Never underestimate the gift of self-confidence. Some people are naturally self-confident, while some have doubts about themselves, their business goals and their dreams. One of the many perks of studying business management is that you will develop more self-esteem, especially if you are doubtful.

You may have all the knowledge and training in the world. However, it all boils down to self-confidence. You may know how to delve into the most complicated project with an intrinsic understanding about how to find the right solution. Nonetheless, you will discover that a lack of self-confidence is a serious impediment to your ultimate success as an entrepreneur. Remember, people are more likely to do business with you and your company if they sense that you have confidence in your talents.

D. MAKING FAVOURABLE IMPRESSIONS ON THE BUSINESS WORLD

Once you decide to become an entrepreneur, you will find that you need to borrow money or attract a group of investors. People are more likely to provide you with needed funds once they learn that you have a degree in business management. You may decide to form a busines partnership. If so, your degree may attract the right person to become your partner. Although a business management degree is not an absolute requirement, it can help give you the boost you need to set your career in motion.

From securing funds to working with the best and most

talented people, one of the advantages of studying management is that you will develop a comprehensive knowledge about the business world.

These are all we will help you achieve at Peak Point School of Business and Management. You may check our website www.peakpointsbm.com for more details.

BASIC STEPS TO TAKE TO CREATE IDENTITY FOR YOUR BUSINESS

If you already have the idea of a business you want to do and understand how you intend to create the value, you may have to consider the following to give your business a unique identity. These exclude essential topics that have been treated in this chapter.

A. HAVING A BUSINESS NAME

One vital branding area for businesses is the name you give your business. The name given to your business should be the type that your proposed clients/customers can easily call and relate with. If possible, it may have to point to what your business entails. Whatever name you call your business, it should not indicate any violence or copy of another existing brand. To ensure your name is recognised by law, you need to proceed to the next stage.

B. REGISTERING YOUR BUSINESS

Corporate Affairs Commission of the Federal Republic of Nigeria is the body that is saddled with the responsibility of registering a business. As mentioned in the previous chapter, the type of your business structure determines the legal approach to the registration. However, the important factor of this stage is that your business name gets secured for you the moment you are registered. This means you can legally operate within the functions you are registered as. This will help you not to get limited.

When doing the registration, make sure your description of what you are doing is considered in your potential expansion in future. This is because once you are registered, it may take too much time and many procedures to get it updated.

C. HAVING TAX IDENTIFICATION NUMBER (TIN)

This is a registration required with the tax authority of your business jurisdiction. It helps you to fulfil the requirements of the Federal Government on tax matters. Understand that this registration does not put you under any immediate obligation to pay tax. If it is a company, you have a grace period of up to 18 months before you can start filling your tax.

Also, the good news is that some of these activities can now be done online. However, to be on the safe side you may engage the tax agent working for SMEs to support you in this aspect, depending on the scale of your business. While at it, you will need your TIN as one of the official requirements for your business documentation in so many places.

D. OPENING A BANK ACCOUNT

After you must have concluded all the above, it is ideal that you open a bank account for your business. This is done to monitor your business transactions more appropriately and to live by the rule that the business exists as an entity that is separate from the owner. Operating with your bank account also positions you well for prospective customers/clients and shows your originality. It helps strangers to easily work with you, especially when they are aware that your data is linked to the file with the federal government.

Other things you may need to consider, which I have

mentioned at some point in this book, are;

- Setting up accounting software for your financial report.
- Identifying your process and procedures and, if possible, getting them documented.
- Setting up your business brand on social media platforms; and
- Creating branding items for the publicity of your business, e.g., banners, flyers etc.

E. RECOGNISING THE GOD-FACTOR

After all is said and done, never forget the place of God in your endeavour. Learn to know Him and understand His words concerning your daily moves, including your business. It takes the grace of God for the seeds a farmer plants to germinate and become ready for harvest.

You need to build a relationship with God and speak to Him about your business. Let Him take the lead in all areas of your life and be sure you are personally connected to Him to discern that He is taking the lead. God, the Giver of all wealth and Rewarder of all diligent work, will not make you labour in vain.

PAST ARTICLES WORTH YOUR READING

ARTICLE 1

OPEN LETTER TO EMPLOYEES THAT ASPIRE ENTREPRENEURSHIP STATUS

I understand you love the "I own my business" claim you hear people make. In fact, it has started appealing to your inner person. However, before you join the "sack your employer gang," be sure you have all it takes. As an employee, you cannot compare yourself to someone who started out as an entrepreneur. They are the only ones whocan tell you the real story of the journey. Everyone owns their story. And no matter how you want to replicate it, it can never be same.

As you learn the ropes of business on the job and prepare for the entrepreneurship status which you cherish so much, you need to remember the following:

- There is a growth period for every success. There is nothing wrong if you desire to disengage from a paid employment to personal business. However, if that is your choice, ensure you are equipped with everything needed for entrepreneurship.

- Financial liberty or freedom is a personal decision which must speak to your personal goals and aspirations. You need to do this to avoid the pitfall thatthose before you in your preferred business were fraught with and that cost them a great deal.

- Work out your own way. Do not depend fully on someone's template. You can use their template as a reference point, which is also a wise approach. Nevertheless, be informed that it may not necessarily work for you the same way it did for them. That is your place of uniqueness.

- They may not tell you all that happens to them behind the scenes. However, for your sanity, be intentional about your approach. There is a difference between plan and actual. That is why we have gap analysis. So, expect gap and be ready to manage it for your growth.

- Be ready to face the challenges and risk in working for yourself. Do not live on successful people's motivational quotes if you cannot push yourself. Change yourself.

- Note that how you take care of others' work will rub off on yours. Trash the myth that says you are working for someone's success. If you work diligently wherever God put you in charge of, you are only helping yourself and, by extension, subtly creating value for yourself. Remember, you are what you have successfully passed through either by responding to challenges, risk or proactively finding solutions to issues.

- There is no dream or goal that can be achieved by self alone. You need people. Most especially, people through whom you pass as you climb up the ladder of life have a way of affirming the value in you. Do not letpride destroy what will help your growth in future. Be good on the job God assigned to you and build a healthy relationship while doing it. You will reap the benefits for life.

- You must have grown your personal value enough to take care of your basic needs before you switch. Do not rush the process. Everyone has their timing. Carefully identify your way and diligently work the journey. Nobody says you should not start before you switch. By the time you leave the 9-5 job, you will have understood all the risks involved in your chosen business. It will also stand as a leveraging ground if anything goes wrong in your prospective business. It will not be as bad as when you do not have anything to leverage. Remember, it is not everyone that has supporting system from family and friends. So, if you are the only one struggling to make your success a sweet one, dare to take the right steps. You cannot afford to have mental health issues when the unexpected happens.

- Know your level of competence and be ready to build yourself. Develop yourself with the vision of your purpose in sight. You must daily see your future in every step you take.
- Be ready to practice delayed gratification. I know a lot of people like to show that they *don hammer*. That may not work when you newly start/switch to your business. It is a different story from when you expect to be paid a monthly salary. So, be ready to build your business by depriving yourself of some luxury lifestyle. This one is deeper than this article can explain.

Finally, you do not have to sack your employer before you grow yourself through your service at work without losing vision. Your desires are achievable if you go through the ideal process.

ARTICLE 2

NEGATIVE MINDSET: THE FIRST ENEMY OF SUCCESS

Your mindset needs to be right for you to be attracted to the right thing you expect or is meant for you. If all you see is negativity, same will be attracted to you. When you fix your mind on possibilities, you get to challenge your current position and will always want to be a better you.

For everyone in business, the following should be your watchword:

- Do not cheat or scam others. There is dignity in labour. There is no greater joy than to enjoy what belongs to you. In other words, up your game by getting the right training for the service you are providing so as to offer outstanding services that will make people refer customers to you.

As a distributor, do not promote what your products cannot offer. Having the right mindset helps you to build trust around you and what you do. Integrity in business is vital to your success.

- Do not hate those who are making progress. Rather, see them as encouragers of who or what you want to become. Learn from them and be a better version of you. When you fix your thoughts, you will see the best of people, which will serve as an opportunity for you to make progress as well. Talk more of collaboration; a lot of people have enjoyed great benefits by collaborating with people in their industries. It is a beautiful business strategy. However, with a shallow mind, this cannot be achieved. So, fix your thoughts.

- See failure as a learning point. It is okay that the decision you make in business or the position you took turned the other way or did not produce the expected results. However, it does not augur well if you fail to analyse the situation and see how you can recover from it.

In business, there is no perfect decision. Therefore, keep reviewing your stand and see how best you need to be as you grow. It may mean that you need to understand what your market needs or other approaches that will hasten the attainment of your goals. It is important that you see failure as a learning strategy so that you can fix your thought.

- Do not engage in unhealthy rivalry that you eat up your investment. Instead of focusing on activities that will make you better in your business based on your business models/progress plans, do not do what you did not plan for, even if others are doing it. If you do without analysing it, you will end up spending your funds on what does not add anything positive to your profitability or brand.

- See God as integral to your activities. This is self-explanatory. If God is not in it, you have not started anything.

Finally, learn to fix your thoughts and see how magical your business and personal life will be.

ARTICLE 3

HOW TO SPEAK THE LANGUAGE OF BUSINESS AND MEASURE YOUR SUCCESS

- Understanding your true WHY.

- Using appropriate strategies that suit your WHY.

- Being consistent with the application of your strategies and review. This is based on target and the extent of the volatility of the industry in which your business operates. Your review may require you to change certain targets or indicate that you move on with the existing ones. However, one of the key things you get from your periodic review is the clarity that you are still in line with your vision.

- Understanding that there is no best strategy. Your WHY (vision and mission) differentiates you from others. Therefore, you must quit being inconsistent in adopting strategies. Find what works best for you.

- Being in the same industry or appearing to be doing the same thing with others. Your true WHY makes you feel fulfilled when you perform the activities attached to your strategy. That is your success.
- Measuring your success with your targets, not with others' achievements. You do this to grow consistently through your targets. However, if you compare your status with others' and discover that it does not measure up, do not let it get to you. If you look at all the necessary factors in setting your target and discover that you are growing, know that you are successful in your own right.

ARTICLE 4

BE ETHIC-DRIVEN

Dear Business Owner or Value Giver,

If you are willing to benefit from online sales channels, be prepared to show YOURSELF ethically. There is something called ethics in all forms of profession, but the principles are the same. Do not forget **PIPCO**, fully explained below.

- **Professional Behaviour:** Always comply with laws/regulations and never discredit your profession.
- **Integrity:** Be straightforward and honest. Do not promise what you cannot deliver.
- **Professional Competence and Due Care:** Maintain professional knowledge and be diligent. Be good at what you say you are offering.
- **Confidentiality**: Do not disclose business information without authorisation or use it to benefit yourself. Some of your clients trust you enough to give out their personal information. Be

careful how you use them. Safeguard them from any form of attacks on their privacy.

- **Objectivity:** Do not allow any form of bias, conflict of interest or undue influence among your staff members. If you have employees working for you, create a business structure. Make your process clear and be the first to comply with it. Let your business culture speak through all you do.

There is more to PIPCO, but I hope you get the gist basedon the summary above. The truth is that nobody knows who you are until you announce yourself by consistently sharing the value in you. You have to give yourself that opportunity to shine. The New International Version of Luke 11:33 says, *"No one lights a lamp and puts it in a place where it will be hidden, or under a bowl. Instead they put it on its stand, so that those who come in may see the light."*

To show up is spiritually inclined. Do not dim your light. Keep it up! Keep shining! My heart desire is to see all businesses thrive.

Much love, Morenike Ogunnowo.

REFERENCES

Business News Daily

JDPC Institute Agricultural Small and Medium Enterprise Investment Scheme Training Manual

CIMA Textbook Manual

https://en.wikipedia.org/

https://www.zendesk.com/

https://getsling.com/

https://smallbusiness.chron.com/

https://www.hiscox.com/

https://community.tefconnect.com/

https://academia.edu.com/

https://smepeaks.com/

https://coursehero.com/

MEET MORENIKE OGUNNOWO

Who is Morenike Ogunnowo?

Morenike Ogunnowo (FCA, CGMA, ACMA) is a seasoned professional accountant with broad experience in financial audit, financial accounting, **financial management**, internal control, corporate governance and **business management,** including human resources and admin management.

She holds a BSc in Business Administration from Olabisi Onabanjo University and became a Chartered Accountant the same year she graduated from university. She was confirmed a Fellow of the Institute of Chartered Accountant of Nigeria (ICAN) about a year ago. She is also a member of Chartered Institute of Management Accountants (CIMA) with Chartered Global Management Accountant (CGMA) and Associate Chartered Management Accountant (ACMA) as her global certifications.

Morenike worked with KPMG Professional Services for over 5 years as a corporate auditor where she took charge and managed assurance engagements of some of the numerous clients of the firm first at the Energy & Natural Resources Section and later at Consumer & Industrial Market Section of the company

About 6 years before this book was published, she joined Honda Manufacturing Nigeria Limited at the executive level. She is currently the Head of Business Management Division with full responsibilities of the Strategic Planning and Management for the company's business, overseeing four departments – Finance; Accounts; Corporate Affairs & IT; and Human Resource & Corporate GovernanceDepartments.

Morenike is also an entrepreneur who understands how to harmonise the impact of business environment in business for optimal efficiency. **She is the CEO of Rennyshouse Services**, a business that has successfully provided products around **fashion and household items** both online and offline. Through Rennyshouse Services, she is out to help fashion distributors solve supply issues without stress.

She is also a co-founder and partner at Ark Partners, an accounting firm that provides financial and management advisory and accountancy services.

She is the principal director at Peak Point School of Business and Management, a business school whose operation is to transfer necessary business knowledge to individuals in businesses and the corporate world.

She is the founder of Pearls of Great Value (PoGV), a platform that brings together women of incorruptible value with the motive to encourage one another in achieving God's purpose. **As godly female/women/mother, members set out to support the youth (both male and female) to focus on what matters and to live in God's purpose by providing them both spiritual and physical aids through PoGV Youth Inspiration Initiative (POYII).**

Over the years, Morenike has displayed dynamic and top-notch leadership skills in several capacities even outside her core roles. She is an advocate of intentional living and this has earned her several opportunities in relationship building. She is currently the Youth Pastor at Upper Room

Brethren Ministry.

She is the beautiful and loving wife of Pastor Adeola Ogunnowo, her husband of 10 years and counting and God blessed their union with two boys and two girls (including a set of twins), Emmanuel, Favour, Joanna (Taiwo) and John (Kehinde).

What was growing up like?

I was born into a very large polygamous family. I grew up under the tutelage of three mothers (my mother inclusive). Despite the polygamous arrangement of my family, my father took education very dearly and that helped a lot of us to break through in life.

I have always been a quiet but industrious person ever since I was in my formative years. I have always loved to turn a naira into another one, an attribute I guess was unconsciously picked from my parents. That made me to venture into several small businesses even when I was progressing in my education at that time. I remember a time my parents had some major challenges in their businesses that made my mother start selling dry fish at the market for almost 3 years or thereabouts.

After school, I would join her and help her to hawk around the market. It was one of the tough moments for them, but their grateful spirit towards life did not allow us (children) to see the challenges. It was really fun making money. I was so happy that phase passed in their life but left me a great lesson. There is no reason to be lazy in life.

My mother was the second wife of my father, while I am the second child of her 3 surviving children and the only surviving girl child among them. In other words, I had an elder brother and a younger brother. One of the saddest periods of my younger age was when I lost my immediate younger brother. He was so dear to me because as young children, we had big pictures about life and were both impacting our immediate environment in our own very little way.

Despite the several challenges and limitations I experienced as a child, I have always lived with a big picture in mind: to make my parents proud of my person on one hand and that I also enjoy life from my legit income. I can say this decision helped me sail through certain challenges of life and helped me to refocus whenever I walk out of my path.

I started and completed my professional examination with the Institute of Chartered Accountant of Nigeria while in university and that helped me to be more positioned for the career path after I finished my NYSC. My decision to start ICAN exam was the work of certain positive-minded individuals around me as well as my willingness to learn and respect to a friend and sister who I got to know was writing the same exam.

I literally did not wait a day after my service year before I resumed work in one of the big 4 accounting firms, KPMG. It was hard work, clarity of purpose and, much more, the grace of God.

As a youth, I was engaged in several activities in church. Choir group, drama group, youth forum, Girls' Guild, Bible quiz forum, ushering department etc. are a few sections of the church administration that I added to my service quota.

As a young girl who loved God, I played a key role in the

evangelical team to publicise and inaugurate St. James' Anglican Church, Molipa, Ijebu Ode, Ogun State, where I also served as the choir leader and youth leader. I was a confirmed member of Anglican Communion as a youth before I got married.

What is more about your career?

As I mentioned earlier, I started my career as a corporate auditor with KPMG Professional services for about 6 years. Before that, I had worked with an ICAN tutorial Institute as senior lecturer, lecturing courses relating to financial accounting, public accounting and taxation.

Lecturing was a part-time job for me as a corps member, as I used my service year as a fund transfer officer with Zenith Bank Plc. I also helped people prepare their business plans or work on their financial plans, all as part-time activities during my service year.

After working for about six years at KPMG, I moved to Honda Manufacturing Nigeria Limited at the executive level as finance adviser and after 6 months of employment, I was confirmed as a member of staff in same company as financial manager. I have since grown in the company to become a senior manager whose work goes beyond managing the

Account and Finance Department to include managing Human Resource and Administration Department.

Today, I am positioned as Chief Finance Officer (CFO) and the Business Management Division Head of the company, where I oversee 4 departments and support in strategic planning, control and risk management for the continuous growth of the business.

What was your passion before you chose Business Management as a career?

Oh my! I think I was graced to have walked in the path that boosted the status I attained. Business Management has always been my passion, especially as a graduate of business administration. However, my professional experience as an auditor helped me to get more hands-on knowledge of the real business world since I had the opportunity to deal and see how different businesses in different industries operate.

So, I will say my experiences, as I grew in my career, helped me to define the status I now find myself. What I only do is to review my plans yearly and re-position myself to the next stage I desire. With this, I had the opportunity to set personal developmental plans for myself and that helped me to feel fulfilled in my chosen career.

What are your thoughts about what it takes to be a professional?

Apart from having the necessary professional certifications that support the professed authority in a chosen career, what distinguishes a professional from others in the same field is the need to diligently follow the **ethics** and values that bind professions. For more on this, you can read up PIPCO (professional behaviour, integrity, professional competence and due care and confidentiality) in the previous chapter. These lend credence to the fact that being a professional goes beyond certification; it is our daily approach to the work we do.

How far does education go with career?

Education is key in all aspect you want to think about it. However, it is important to note that the application of our knowledge is much more valuable. So, beyond your educational qualification, be ready to impact and add value to your business by being flexible, proactive and innovative to adapt to your volatile business environment.

You need to continuously get trained and develop yourself as the business environment changes so as to be relevant and ready to make timely and valuable decision. To effectively contribute value in any chosen career, you need to be adequately informed in more than one profession. This will have impact on factors that play out in the business environment and beyond.

If, at this point, Nigeria diversifies from oil production to agriculture, will it have a positive impact on the economy?

There is more to be done as a country if we need the agriculture sector to produce the real result expected. I believe there is more to providing funds through grants and other means, two of which are gathering of data and monitoring of activities that have yet to be explored at the expected level in my view. If we can make do with the necessity in this aspect, Agriculture sector can yield positive impact on our economy.

As a country, we have the necessary major resources to achieve this, but there are several secondary resources-- especially in technology-- that have yet to be public knowledge to players in this field.

Agriculture is already gaining ground, as there are several areas in the industry that the masses can play in. Regrettably, these areas have yet to be maximised partly because of limited knowledge and the inaccessibility of players to necessary infrastructure.

In all, if we can get agro-related businesses right, we can create more opportunities for exportation and create more jobs for many citizens and non-citizens, leading to less reliance on FX needs to take care of the basic needs of the country.

All these are positive impacts on the country's economy.

Why should the masses choose RENNYHOUSE?

RENNYSHOUSE SERVICES is a thriving registered business enterprise that deals in the sales of fashion items and accessories such as shoes, wristwatches, jewellery, clothing etc. at very affordable and discounted wholesale prices.

We pride ourselves in being the best at offering great deals in the fashion industry. We belong to a distinguished class of fashion industry with a clearly defined market path across Nigeria.

Our footprints are also clearly visible in the areas of prompt delivery service at friendly charges, selling quality and durable products and promoting good customer relation, with our rapid growth proving these outstanding qualities as consistently shown by our excellent team of professionals.

Our tagline is **quality and affordability**, an affirmation of the excellent service we provide in terms of distribution of fashion items and connecting with a larger audience in our bid to fulfil our vision and mission.

Since inception, Rennyshouse Services has successfully provided fashion and household products. These products are geared towards getting feedback from existing and prospective customers as to what measures their satisfaction.

Major areas of strength of Rennyshouse Services are:

- **Quality at affordable price**: We provide goods and services at affordable prices without compromising quality.

- **Integrity**: Through our actions and communication, honesty is established. And this has built trust with our existing customers and boosted customer retention over the years.

- **Open communication**: Our lines of communication are open and we respond timely to all our customers.

OUR OBJECTIVE

Our core objective is to encourage and stand as a support system for individuals and SMEs and contribute to value chain appreciation, especially in the fashion distribution industry.

OUR VISION

To maintain a trusted channel for the supplies of quality fashion items at affordable prices.

OUR MISSIONS

1. To get the youth and qualified adults engaged in value creation through distribution of fashion items.

2. To create an enabling channel for the working class to have multiple streams of income.

3. To be the go-to fashion outfit for budding fashion distributors and make them grow without fear.

4. To source quality products that will position our target's reputation positively in their market.

5. To provide advice appropriate for the growth of all stakeholders in fashion distribution channels.

7. To efficiently provide great service to our customers by giving appropriate knowledge and values to our employees; and

6. To become a household name in the fashion distribution industry.

WHERE WE ARE

- We have launched and have been operating in product lines for distribution of shoes, wristwatches, jewelries and children's clothing to wholesalers and distributors.
- We strengthen our operations by engaging proven staff members that attend to distributors and make on-time delivery.
- We have created a business structure and positioned our warehouse/showroom in a way that makes operations easier.
- We serve our wholesalers/distributors both physically and online.
- Our online channels of distribution are WhatsApp, Telegram and websites. We use our Instagram and Facebook pages to engage our existing customers and attract prospective customers to our brand. Effective from January 2021, our customers (both wholesalers and distributors) can now reach out to us and place their order through our website www.rennyshousewholesale.com.
- We provide clear product pictures to aid sales for our customers who sell online.

- We have grown our customer base over the years.
- Although we have done so much, we need to actively engage our prospective customers as we have not fully captured our targeted market.

As a business woman and career lady, how do you balance career and business with family?

I learnt how to prioritise tasks early in my career. This has immensely helped me in managing my time and to-dos in all aspects of my life.

I love to prepare the family meal except when we have timeout as family or when I am unavoidably out of the house.

As a family, we concluded not to have a maid or steward. So, I learn how to manage the little available time between my schedules for issues relating to family that need my attention. Because of this, I can conveniently plan a huge function remotely without too much contact with vendors.

I must also say that the support of my husband is vital to my personal growth. Over the years, he has consistently allowed me to be the person I am today while being a great help in building our marriage and home. Being a pastor does not stop him from being a great comfort and my number one fan.

At some point in my career, I worked and managed to achieve a work-life balance. This got easier as I grew in it. There were times our relations came around to stay with us to provide support.

Today, my kids understand my work and I create time to hear from them. I allow them to talk to me when I am available and I also communicate all I do to them, even when it appears they do not understand.

In all, God has been faithful.

Who is your mentor?

I honestly do not have any person to call a direct mentor at present. However, I have always built good relationship with people. This has helped me get attention on matters that I need clarification on.

Once in a while, I chat with some people above me in career path who I hold in high esteem and open my mind to a lot of things that birth some of the things I do. I also have people that I study from distance. I call them my role models. The number one on my current list is Ibukun Awosika. Most times, I see myself in her. Even though we have not met, I see her results mirroring the kind of person I am becoming.

Spiritually, I can say confidently that the Holy Spirit has been a great inspiration to a lot of values I have today. I was made perfect in Him.

How can existing or prospective customers connect with you?

I would love to get feedback on how this book has added value to you. You can reach out to me on:

Facebook: Morenike Ogunnowo
Instagram: Morenike Ogunnowo
E-mail: morenike.ogunnowo@gmail.com
Telegram: Morenike Ogunnowo

LinkedIn: Morenike Ogunnowo

To connect with my businesses:

Rennyshouse Services: www.rennyshousewholesale.com

Peak Point School of Business and Management: www.peakpointsbm.com

www.ingramcontent.com/pod-product-compliance
Lightning Source LLC
Chambersburg PA
CBHW052352220526
45465CB00003BA/1068